# THE LEARNED DISCIPLINES OF MANAGEMENT

# THE LEARNED DISCIPLINES OF MANAGEMENT

## HOW TO MAKE THE RIGHT THINGS HAPPEN

JIM BURKETT

MANAGEMENT PRESS.

THE LEARNED DISCIPLINES OF MANAGEMENT. Copyright © 2014 by Jim Burkett. All rights reserved. Printed in the United States of America. No part of this book may be used or reproduced, distributed, or transmitted in any manner or by any means, including photocopying, recording, or other electronic and mechanical methods without the prior written permission of the publisher except in the case of brief quotations embodied in critical articles and reviews and certain other noncommercial uses permitted by copyright law. For permission requests, write to the publisher at: Management Press, Inc., P.O. Box 127, Bath, Ohio 44210.

Management Press and the Management Press logo are trademarks of Management Press, Inc.

Ordering Information

Individual Sales. Management Press books are available in bookstores. They can also be ordered directly from Management Press: for electronic ordering visit www.mgtpress.com or write to the publisher at the above address.

Quantity sales. Special discounts are available on quantity purchases by corporations, associations, college textbook or course applications and other organizations. To order electronically visit www.mgtpress.com or write to the publisher at the above address.

Also available as an e-book

FIRST EDITION

Publisher's Cataloging-In-Publication Data

Burkett, Jim, 1954-
  The learned disciplines of management : how to make the right things happen / Jim Burkett. -- 1st ed.

  p. : forms ; cm.

  Includes bibliographical references and index.
  ISBN: 978-0-9895170-0-3

  1. Management--Evaluation. 2. Executive ability. 3. Performance. 4. Organizational change. I. Title.

HD31 .B87 2014
658.4                                                                                          2013942342

This book is dedicated to my beautiful wife and best friend Roslyn, my three delightful children; Elliot, Ethan and Kiera, and most importantly to God who is the giver of all good things.

Soli Deo Gloria

"To God alone the praise be given for what's herein to man's use written."

—Johann Sebastian Bach

# Contents

| | |
|---|---|
| *Preface* | *viii* |
| Introduction | 1 |
| 1: Planning | 23 |
| 2: Organizing | 42 |
| 3: Measuring Performance | 64 |
| 4: Executing | 93 |
| 5: Following Up | 114 |
| 6: Real-Time Reporting | 134 |
| 7: Problem Solving | 154 |
| 8: Deploying the Disciplines | 170 |
| Appendix A: Management: A Calling | 196 |
| Appendix B: Typical Departmental Performance Ratios | 210 |
| Notes | 213 |
| Index | 216 |

# Preface

# What's in YOUR tool kit?

Perhaps it's prevailing management theory taught by respected academics. Or it may be the latest management fad. Your tool kit may hold management techniques passed on by your predecessor or management methods given to you by your boss.

But are they the right tools? Are they tools that make you effective—tools that allow you to make the right things happen? In other words, does your tool kit hold the seven learned disciplines of management? Your tool kit must include the following tools:

 *Planning:* This management discipline determines the right aims and the necessary means to achieve them.

 *Organizing:* This management discipline orders how activities are performed so as to maximize results and optimize resources.

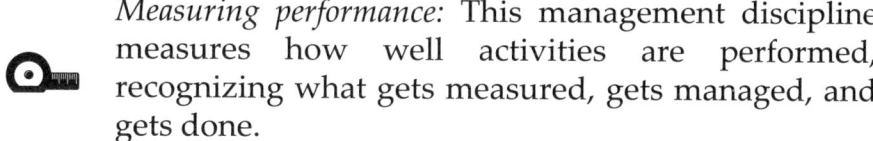

*Measuring performance:* This management discipline measures how well activities are performed, recognizing what gets measured, gets managed, and gets done.

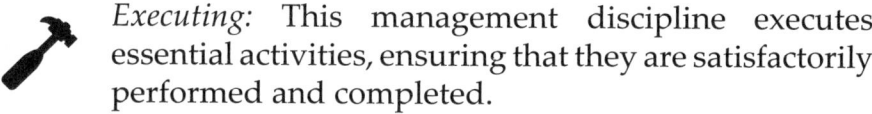

*Executing:* This management discipline executes essential activities, ensuring that they are satisfactorily performed and completed.

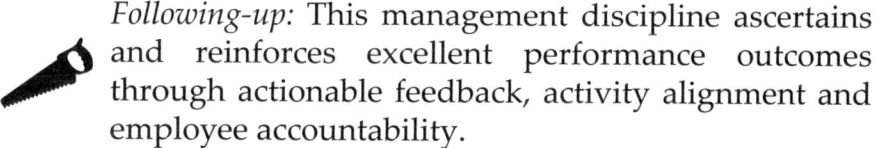

*Following-up:* This management discipline ascertains and reinforces excellent performance outcomes through actionable feedback, activity alignment and employee accountability.

*Real-time reporting:* This management discipline circulates real-time performance information throughout the organization to facilitate making the right things happen.

*Problem solving:* This management discipline uses actionable feedback to identify, understand, and solve problems.

If you find that your management tool kit is lacking, don't despair. Every one of the disciplines can be learned and in *The Learned Disciplines of Management* you will discover how to use them to make the right things happen.

# THE LEARNED DISCIPLINES OF MANAGEMENT

# Introduction

> We should remember that one man is much the same as another, and that he is best who is trained in the severest school.
>
> —Thucydides

It is mind-boggling to consider that only one hundred fifty years ago (about the time of the American Civil War) armed conflict was carried out using hand-loaded, black-powdered muskets and cannons. There were no antibiotics and no modern vaccines or drugs. Surgery, when attempted at all, was a primitive, bare-handed affair that often ended in death, and dentistry was an inadvertent form of torture. The sharing of information over long distances mainly took place through handwritten letters delivered in the mail and the occasional telegram. Animal power, especially horses, provided the primary means for land transportation, while wind power was the chief means for water transport.

Since then, we have seen an unprecedented explosion of innovation. Warfare is now carried out using machine guns, tanks, aircraft carriers, supersonic jets, laser-guided missiles, and unmanned drones.

The field of medicine has seen the advance of antibiotics, modern vaccines, and pharmaceutical drugs. Surgeries are conducted using sterile operating techniques in operating theaters packed with high-tech equipment, and most dentistry procedures are routine inconveniences.

Today, information is shared using telephones, radios, televisions, cell phones, and personal computers, replacing the telegraph and eclipsing the handwritten letter.

The internal combustion engine is today's prime mover, powering autos, trucks, locomotives, and ships (not to mention nuclear reactors that power naval submarines and aircraft carriers). Finally, there is powered flight, something we take for granted today but was inconceivable one hundred fifty years ago. It has transformed transportation, enabling travel around our planet and beyond.

In the past century and a half, these advancements (and countless others) have been planned, developed, produced, and distributed, changing our lives. Yet these innovations could not have come into reality and made so readily available without another innovation—one that management theorist and writer Peter Drucker considered "the most important innovation" of the twentieth century—management.[1]

Webster's dictionary defines management as "the act or art of managing," the "judicious use of means to accomplish an end."[2] But how is this done? How are managers able to judiciously use resources to successfully accomplish a desired end?

Answering this question addresses the management innovation that Peter Drucker refers to. For management's successful results do not simply occur, nor do they continue without managers practicing certain fundamental management disciplines that enable managers to make the right things happen.

A manager's ability to make the right things happen is not an innate skill—no one is born a manager. Although management does require certain aptitudes (in appendix A, I explore assessing one's management aptitude), it also requires learning certain disciplines. Once these management disciplines are learned, their practice is made usable, durable, and instinctive. Now the management disciplines function as tools that extend a manager's skill, allowing the manager to accomplish more than would have been possible without these tools.

What are the learned disciplines of management? There are seven. They provide a coherent framework of individual disciplines that are linked together to form a powerful, self-reinforcing management system for making the right things happen. They include planning, organizing, measuring performance, executing, following up, real-time reporting, and problem solving. Each discipline is impactful, and all are indispensable. Their practice is the best way to understand what effective management does.

The first management discipline is *planning*. The practice of this discipline determines the right aims and the necessary means to achieve them.

The second management discipline is *organizing*. Practicing this discipline orders how activities are performed so as to optimize resources and maximize results.

*Measuring performance* is the third management discipline. The practice of this discipline measures how well activities are performed, recognizing what gets measured, gets managed, and gets done.

The fourth management discipline is *executing*. Practicing this discipline executes essential activities, ensuring that they are satisfactorily performed and completed.

*Following up* is the fifth management discipline. Its practice ascertains and reinforces excellent performance outcomes through actionable feedback, activity alignment and employee accountability.

The sixth management discipline is *real-time reporting*. Practicing this discipline circulates real-time performance information throughout the organization to facilitate making the right things happen.

The seventh and final management discipline is *problem solving*. Its practice uses actionable feedback to identify, understand, and solve problems.

Solving problems, and hence making the right things happen, is the hallmark of effective management. Therefore, management's capacity to make the right things happen is multiplied when the seven learned disciplines of management are practiced.

When management lacks these tools, their effectiveness

is diminished, which allows the wrong things to happen. Murphy's Law states, "Anything that can go wrong will go wrong." In organizations that allow the wrong things to happen, management requires more of everything—more employees, more materials, more equipment, more money, and so on—to produce the same or diminished results. Left unchecked, the wrong things proliferate, causing organizations to wallow in mediocrity or flounder in failure.

The results of management struggling to make the right things happen include, for example, graduating students who cannot read, manufactured products that don't work, medical treatment that harms patients, service employees who don't serve, salespeople who can't sell, equipment that kills troops sent in harm's way, sports teams that don't win, police officers who cannot shoot straight, and managers who cannot produce a profit. These examples and countless others illustrate management's inability to skillfully practice the learned disciplines of management and make the right things happen.

But if skillfully practicing the learned disciplines of management is so essential to management success, why is it not done? Why are mediocre results so prevalent, and why is management success so elusive? To help answer these questions, we turn to a nineteenth-century military theorist named Carl von Clausewitz, who wrote, "Everything is very simple in War, but the simplest thing is difficult."[3]

What von Clausewitz observed about war is true of management as well. The disciplines that encompass management practice are simple in themselves, but carrying them out produces a kind of friction or inertia that makes practicing them difficult. These difficulties cause the disciplines not to be practiced at all or to be practiced ineffectively, resulting in managers who stumble along in frustration and failure.

There are three main reasons the learned disciplines of management are not practiced effectively. The first reason is management's lack of knowledge. Many managers don't know that their management effectiveness depends on practicing the seven learned disciplines of management (this was my own experience managing). Therefore, managers neglect the disciplines.

The second reason is that managers don't know how to use the learned disciplines of management pragmatically. Consequently, managers misuse the disciplines.

The third reason is that managers do not know how to use the learned disciplines of management systematically. When the disciplines are not practiced systematically, management has no assurance they will be used integrally, constantly, and consistently.

Your management effectiveness depends on learning and skillfully practicing the learned disciplines of management. Therefore, think of this book as a management training camp where managers at all levels are taught how to master the learned disciplines of management. The approach to teaching these disciplines is similar to a training camp conducted many years ago on a hot and dusty field in Green Bay, Wisconsin.

In 1959, the Green Bay Packers hired Vince Lombardi as their head coach and general manager. The team was a dismal failure, having won only one game during the 1958 season and having posted eleven consecutive losing seasons (the Packers hadn't had a winning season since 1947). Revamping the Packers' football program became Lombardi's job.

Lombardi's approach was basic—teach the game's fundamental disciplines. He used this basic approach beginning in his first Packers' training camp (and every training camp thereafter).

Holding a football in his hand, he began, "Gentlemen, this is a football."[4]

He did this not to belittle his players but to impart his belief that when they mastered the fundamental football disciplines, they would be effective and successful. His lecture was to both grizzled veterans and rookies alike. (One veteran joked, "Uh,

Coach, could you slow down a little. You're going too fast for us?"[5]) In front of him sat some of the world's best athletes and highest-paid football players. They had played football since they were children and now as men and years later, some of them would be inducted into the Pro Football Hall of Fame, along with their coach.

In addition to the football's size and shape, Lombardi went on to explain how a football could be kicked, carried, or passed. He discussed the game's rules and procedures. He took the team out onto the field and walked them around, describing its dimensions and shape. He broke down every position's performance characteristics and then demonstrated how each position interacted and supported the others.

For Lombardi, stressing the fundamental disciplines was not a onetime thing. It was not only how he began each training camp, but it was also how he conducted every practice and every game. He did this even after the Green Bay Packers became a class unto themselves. They won six divisional titles and five NFL championships in an eight-year period (without ever posting a losing record) and achieved victories in Super Bowls I and II.

Lombardi's approach to coaching football was validated, as his Packers are regarded as one of the greatest football dynasties in NFL history. And Lombardi is recognized as one of the finest football coaches of all time.

Similarly, to enhance your management effectiveness, I am going to teach the fundamentals of management. They encompass disciplines whose mastery empowers your success. This book is not another tome discussing management theory. Instead, it emphasizes the practical over the academic. It stresses indispensable and timeless principles rather than the latest fad. When finished, you will have at your disposal a comprehensive system of management practice that will enable you to make the right things happen.

To help you master the learned disciplines of management,

each discipline will be explained and its unique capabilities demonstrated using actual job cases drawn from my thirty-five-year management career. Additionally, you will learn how to use the disciplines systematically, to ensure their constant and comprehensive practice. Having a system for managing is vital because it prevents the disciplines from being practiced inconsistently (or not at all), which produces flawed outcomes and uneven results.

Early in my career as a fledgling manager, at a Fortune 500 company that manufactured passenger tires, I did not realize that the seven learned disciplines of management were instrumental to my management effectiveness. Nor did I appreciate that these disciplines had to be practiced systematically. It was not until I was hired by a management consulting firm and assigned to help a struggling Illinois manufacturing plant that I was able to recognize the essential nature of the seven learned disciplines.

A Fortune 500 company had hired the management consulting firm I worked for to help improve one of their underperforming manufacturing divisions. I was one among four other consultants assigned to the project. To accomplish the project's aim, our consulting team had to find ways to improve how the plant's various departments performed. I was assigned the plant's Cell Subassembly Department. This was not a promising assignment, as cell subassembly was considered the plant's biggest headache.

Over the years, the department had garnered the reputation of being the plant's chief bottleneck and source of its problems. This department manufactured cells, subassemblies that, when completed, were sent to Final Assembly to be placed into a larger unit called a motor control (motor controls make up the electrical infrastructure of large buildings, controlling elevators, electrical motors, and other heavy electrical equipment).

The Cell Subassembly Department struggled to produce the right kinds of cells in the proper quantities. This affected Final Assembly's ability to complete a customer's motor control unit, limiting the number of motor controls that were shipped. This limitation contributed to the plant's ongoing struggle to make a profit, a struggle that would soon end, for the plant was to be closed if it could not be made profitable.

The Cell Subassembly Department's poor results were not for lack of trying. There had been many well-meaning attempts to try and improve the department's performance over the years. But a constant stream of new hires, added work shifts, and endless overtime failed to produce enough cells and only further eroded profitability. Now it was my turn to try and remedy the situation.

I spent six weeks embedded in the Cell Subassembly Department. My job was to study how the department operated, scrutinizing how it could be managed better. Relying on my recent training as a newly minted management consultant, I analyzed how the department's various activities were performed. This process allowed me to design a system for managing the department. The system consisted of a handful of management disciplines my employer had trained me to use — supposed tools whose practice would make the department's management more effective.

When the six weeks came to an end, I was asked to give our client's executives a formal presentation. During the presentation, I was expected to share what I had observed in the department and offer recommendations to improve the department's performance and profitability. We met in a conference room where I launched confidently into the presentation. My confidence had little to do with my cell manufacturing experience (my six weeks compared to the company's twenty-five years) but rather because I had seen how mismanaged the department was. I began detailing all the problems I had observed — all the wrong things management had allowed to happen.

The problems I chronicled were an embarrassment to our clients. In response, they demanded to know more specific details about the problems so that they could intervene. Although this was a natural reaction, I pointed out that their desire to intervene was shortsighted and would be short-lived, since the problems I had identified were only examples of the deep-seated, systemic problems that took place in the department every day. Instead, I suggested a different approach was needed to address the problems. The approach systematically applied fundamental management disciplines—disciplines, I emphasized, that the Cell Subassembly management were not practicing at all.

Continuing my presentation, I recommended implementing just such a system, one I had custom-tailored for the Cell Subassembly Department. I went on to explain how the management system worked to improve a manager's effectiveness. Additionally, I recommended reorganizing the department and laid out plans that would maximize resources and results.

Our clients nodded agreeably. So far they saw nothing in my recommendations to contradict what they believed needed to be done. However, this amicable response was about to abruptly change as I came to my last and most controversial recommendation.

Mustering as much bravado as I could, I stated, "Once these recommended changes are implemented, it will require far fewer employees to staff the department. Based on my analysis, there will no longer be a need for fifty-five first-shift assemblers. There will no longer be a need for the second shift and its twenty assemblers. There will no longer be a need for overtime. As our client executives squirmed in their seats I added: "Starting next week, assuming all of my recommendations are implemented, I propose employing only seventy-five assemblers, instead of the current one hundred fifty, to operate the Cell Subassembly Department. Seventy-five assemblers are all we will need (including vacation and absentee time) to meet the plant's current production demands."

I'll never forget the looks on their faces as I concluded my presentation. There was a very long, awkward moment of silence before expressions started to register. Their speechlessness was a result of their utter shock, and their expressions reflected a stunned astonishment that grew into angry disbelief and disdain.

In their defense, it should be pointed out that the presenter (me) was a recent college graduate with only nine months' work experience (garnered mostly in my first job out of college supervising passenger tire production). Furthermore, I had no experience manufacturing electrical equipment except the recent six weeks spent observing the Cell Subassembly Department. This was miniscule compared to the department managers' collective experience (totaling over forty years).

In fact, their reaction was not unexpected. My own consulting colleagues had the same reaction when I first shared my initial findings and recommendations with them in preparing for my client presentation. They too were certain I was wrong. However, unlike our clients, they had good reason to suspect my conclusions knowing how inexperienced I was. This practice presentation was a painful, long-drawn-out affair where I had to thoroughly defend my facts and conclusions.

In defending my conclusions, I strictly held to the formal training I had received. Nevertheless, I was told to recheck my facts and to confirm my conclusions using only hard numbers and observable data and avoiding any assumptions. With this additional effort, I was finally able to convince my consulting colleagues that I had arrived at the seemingly correct recommendations. Only then was I allowed to move forward and present them to our client's executives. But my boss had made it clear that if my recommendations were not correct, I'd be fired and sent packing.

My contention was that the Cell Subassembly Department's managers were not practicing the learned disciplines of management. There was no planning for specific results; rather, management simply reacted to one crisis after the next. The department was poorly organized and wasting resources. Performance was not measured and was not being managed. There was no effective execution, which resulted in essential activities being carried out haphazardly. Not practicing these disciplines prevented effectual follow-up, making management incapable of constructively impacting performance. Without effective follow-up, there was no real-time reporting (instead, "reporting" consisted of monthly accounting information) with which to take corrective action. Not practicing these six management disciplines made practicing the seventh, problem solving, a futile effort. And one of the many costly consequences of management not solving problems was having to employ seventy-five more assemblers than was necessary.

Once our client's executives regained their composure, the most they would agree to was a test. I would like to think that it was my persuasiveness as a presenter that swayed them to even consider my recommendations. But the fact was that after years of trying to improve the department's performance, nothing had worked. Now they were desperate, willing to try anything. If I was wrong, the necessary productivity improvements would not materialize and the plant would be closed, costing hundreds of jobs (including my own).

The agreed-on test allowed for the Cell Subassembly Department to be reorganized along the lines I had recommended. However, rather than lay off seventy-five assemblers, management insisted they be assigned "cleaning duties" in the adjoining department. Given management's many failed attempts at improving the department's performance, the plant's executives were certain my plan would fail too. If it did, they wanted the furloughed assemblers readily available to quickly rejoin the department. They were certain a frantic call for more assemblers would come after only a short time.

The following Monday morning (after a weekend spent hurriedly reorganizing the department), the remaining seventy-five assemblers, their supervisors, and I gathered. A supervisor reviewed all the changes that had been made to the department—changes, it was explained, that would help improve how the department performed. It was hoped, the supervisor went on, that these changes would allow for fewer assemblers who would produce even more cells—enough cells, in fact, to keep the plant's Final Assembly Department adequately supplied.

One of the assemblers spoke up. Looking around at the diminished number of assemblers, he mockingly exclaimed, "Yeah, right!" His skepticism was understandable. This was not the first time management had attempted to improve the department's performance. But of all the attempts, this one seemed to him the most desperate and futile yet. I am sure he was not alone in his opinion.

A deep sense of apprehension began to sink in as I looked into the faces of the gathered employees. Were we expecting too much? Was this indeed a desperate act that would end in failure? Could the department's performance really be improved—dramatically—by simply practicing the seven fundamental management disciplines?

I had a growing sense of foreboding, which was easy to understand, for I honestly did not know whether the learned disciplines of management would work. You see, I had no experience actually using them. Although I had been employed at the consulting firm for a few months, this time had been spent in training, first at the firm's training center and then on-site at various clients' consulting projects. But even during my training, I never imagined being placed in a situation like this. Could I pull it off? Would the management disciplines work? Would they really help the Cell Subassembly managers make the right things happen?

These questions would be answered shortly. I struggled to suppress my feelings of self-doubt and not be overwhelmed at the challenges ahead. I busily threw myself into my first implementation of the learned disciplines of management. It would be here in cell subassembly that I would see firsthand the results of practicing them and the effect they had on management effectiveness and success. Tellingly, it would not be the last.

Chaos, confusion, and conflict initially marked practicing the learned disciplines of management. The incidents that unfolded shocked and distressed me, further deepening my anxiety. It was only later that I came to realize that these were sure indications the learned disciplines of management were working, but at the time, I thought I had created a perpetual mess.

Numerous and varied problems were uncovered. These were problems that until now had gone unrecognized and unidentified. At first, the sheer multitude of the problems overwhelmed the Cell Subassembly managers, adding to the chaos and confusion. But as they slowly began to address the problems (based on the extensive feedback they were now receiving), employee performance started to improve. Soon there was a small but a growing rhythm of much needed progress.

We knew this objectively. Two hours after we began practicing the learned disciplines of management, we had generated real-time performance information. This information told us how each assembler performed (and cumulatively how the department performed) while documenting the reasons why productivity was so low, thus enabling management to identify, understand, and address the problems.

What improvements we eked out that first day (including not having to call on the other seventy-five assemblers waiting to come to our rescue) was added to the next day's progress. The first week ended, and the results were okay but far from ideal. It was clear that many problems had eroded the department's productivity, resulting in costly overtime. The one bright spot was we *almost* met the week's cell production requirements.

Progress continued the next week, through problems being

identified and effectively solved. Consequently, the seventy-five assemblers' productivity continued to improve. The second week ended without any overtime. But the seeming unending problems had once again affected the department's performance, resulting in not enough cells being produced.

The third week marked a minor milestone as our seventy-five assemblers, without any overtime, produced the required number of cells. But this milestone was soon eclipsed the following week as even more cells were produced. When the fourth week's cell production was combined, we had set a new monthly production record. This monthly record represented the most cells ever produced in the department's twenty-five-year history.

But that record did not last long. The following month, even more cells were produced, setting a new cell production record—a record that once again was broken the next month as the department's performance began to level off.

Unexpectantly, we faced another challenge. At the department's rear, where the completed cells were staged for the Final Assembly Department, was a mountain of finished cells. I had never seen so many, nor had anyone else. There were so many cells that we had run out of room to stage and store them. As they continued to pile up, we had to have them trucked to another area to be stored.

The reason was clear. Final Assembly had yet to begin practicing the learned disciplines of management. Consequently, this department could not keep up because its productivity was much lower than our newly reconstituted Cell Subassembly Department. Shockingly, for the first time, Final Assembly—not Cell Subassembly—was the plant's new bottleneck.

Practicing the learned disciplines of management in the Cell Subassembly Department increased cell production and reduced operating costs by over 50 percent. The learned disciplines of management were also implemented and practiced in the plant's other departments. Here too productivity increased while reducing operating costs (between 10 and 30 percent) as managers became more proficient at making the right things happen. Management's transformation put an end to talks about closing the plant. Ironically, a plant that had struggled for years to make a profit was now held out as an example for the company's other divisions to follow.

This experience provided a seminal moment in my management career. It validated the essential nature of the learned disciplines of management as I got to see firsthand how they impacted management effectiveness. These early experiences filled a knowledge void in how management made the right things happen, providing me the tools that would bolster my future management success. Thanks to this success, I was able to start my own management consulting firm, which specializes in turning around troubled companies.

Consequently, my experiences at these two consulting firms honed my knowledge of how to practice the learned disciplines of management and have made this book possible. Because these experiences are central to this book, I'd like to elaborate on them for you.

I was hired as a management consultant very early in my management career. At the time, I was a recent college graduate employed at a Fortune 500 company that manufactured passenger tires. I was a production supervisor over the Green Tire Department. This department processed passenger tires and then transported them to the curing presses. During my brief tenure at the company, I had significantly improved my department's performance. This small achievement caught the attention of a management recruiter.

An East Coast management consulting firm had retained the recruiter. The consulting firm specialized in improving management effectiveness at large (mainly Fortune 500) companies. The firm was looking for accomplished managers to recruit as possible consulting candidates. The candidates would be tested, interviewed, and evaluated. Should they pass muster, they would be hired as management consultants for the firm's growing practice.

The recruiter took me through several preliminary interviews and then turned me over to the consulting firm's managers and executives, who thrust me into an extensive (three aptitude tests and seven interviews) and convoluted (psychological profiling, handwriting analysis, and high-pressure grilling tactics) interviewing process. Finally, after many weeks, the process came to an end and I was invited to join the firm.

I was elated with my newfound profession. I was now a management consultant, and my colleagues were other consultants, experts in enhancing management's effectiveness. The firm's client list included some of the most respected companies in the world, representing all sorts of industries. As a young man set on a management career, the opportunity to gain such varied and valuable experience was a dream come true (only later would I come to fully appreciate what an invaluable and matchless experience this was).

The consulting firm I joined was steeped in employing certain methods to make management more effective. The methods included developing, designing, and implementing a system for managing that incorporated a handful of management disciplines. Practicing these disciplines enabled management to maximize resources and results while carrying out essential activities, resulting in reduced operating expenses and increased profits.

As consultants trained to employ our firm's methods, we found that actually implementing our recommendations was the most crucial and challenging aspect of our work. Our firm's approach was different from many other consulting firms who rely on client management to implement their recommendations. Unfortunately, these recommendations (presented in a nicely bound book) are rarely implemented as the book sits on a shelf collecting dust.

Although our firm made recommendations to clients

(presented too in a nicely bound book), our work did not end there. We were expected to implement the recommendations alongside client management. This implementation phase was so crucial, intense, and time consuming that it usually took up the bulk of the consulting project's billable hours.

A typical consulting project had three or four consultants assigned to it and would last several months. During that time, I would develop, design, and implement the learned disciplines of management in various departments—for example, a purchasing department, followed by an engineering department, a customer service department, and an operating department—while my colleagues did the same in other assigned departments. When the consulting project concluded, I was placed on other client projects in various industries and specialized departments throughout the United States and Europe.

Each consulting project promised clients significant results, thus justifying our exorbitant fees. And produce results we did. Our consultants, employing the firm's methods, despite the kind of industry or department specialization, normally produced operational improvements and documented profit savings ranging between 10 and 20 percent (sometimes more, as illustrated in the cell subassembly example). In each instance, practicing the learned disciplines of management transformed management effectiveness, enabling managers to make the right things happen.

These results had a profound impact on my ability to recognize how important it was for management to practice the fundamental management disciplines. Prior to joining the consulting firm, if you had asked me to identify these disciplines and to explain how they were carried out in the real world, I could not have done so.

My inability to answer these questions was not because I was a dim-witted student of management or an incompetent manager. By this stage in my management career, I had a business management degree from a highly regarded state university. Additionally, as already noted, I had achieved some success in my first job out of college managing at a Fortune 500 company, which led to an elite, international management consulting firm hiring me.

Yet, despite these advantages, I could not have named the seven essential management disciplines. Neither could I explain how they were used individually nor collectively in a system for managing. Furthermore, if you had suggested that I could enhance management effectiveness across diverse industries and various departmental specialties, but without any specific industry knowledge or specialized departmental expertise, I would have considered the suggestion naive. Finally, if you had stated I could, without any prior experience, dramatically improve an organization's performance and profitability (where existing management, with years of specialized experience, had tried but failed to do) through a simple system of management practice, I would have considered you delusional.

As it turned out, these assumptions were neither naive nor delusional. But it took seeing the learned disciplines of management practiced many times, in many kinds of situations, before I became convinced otherwise.

Eventually I left the consulting firm. But I was grateful for the knowledge and experience I had obtained. I had been indoctrinated into practicing the learned disciplines of management and was experienced in using them in all kinds of industries and departmental specialties. This knowledge and experience would prove indispensable in managing my own management consulting firm.

In 1987, I founded Corporate Turnaround Consulting, Inc., which specializes in operational turnarounds of underperforming and troubled companies, a subspecialty of the management consulting profession. Turning around troubled companies would demonstrate in an even more remarkable and unique way how essential the practice of the learned disciplines of management is to management success. For a troubled company's plight epitomizes dysfunctional management and scarce and dwindling resources. It would be against these dire conditions that the learned disciplines of management were practiced, testing whether they could quickly produce the necessary results.

Thucydides, an ancient Greek historian, insightfully said, "We should remember that one man is much the same as another, and that he is best who is trained in the severest school."[6] The venue that has been the "severest school" in my management training has been turning around troubled companies. These experiences have been a crucible not only in testing the capabilities of the learned disciplines of management but also in helping me understanding their practice in a deeper, more profound way.

Turning around a failing company has one aim: survival. The turnaround process is analogous to the work an emergency room surgeon performs. The surgeon's one aim is to save a patient's life and first requires that the surgeon quickly and skillfully evaluate a dying patient's condition. This evaluation leads to identifying and prioritizing the necessary medical treatment that must be carried out. Once this course has been determined, the surgeon has a limited amount of time and resources (the patient's bodily resources) to skillfully perform lifesaving surgery.

Turning around troubled companies entails these same dynamics. There is the need, amid limited time and resources, to find and fix the problems that are causing the company's imminent demise. These circumstances compel quick action, especially confronting the discredited attempts of previous managers to make the right things happen—efforts they were either unable or unwilling to do.

Added to this dysfunctional muddle are apathetic and disillusioned employees, hostile and threatening vendors, unhappy and hesitant customers, wary bankers disinclined to make further loans and unwilling to ignore violated loan covenants, and demoralized stakeholders who face losing their invested capital, income source, and any personal assets they have pledged as loan guarantees.

Cash—the lifeblood of business enterprise—and time are a troubled company's most scarce resources, imperiling its future. Consequently, the turnaround practitioner must quickly evaluate the company's condition and take action to stop the cash losses. This includes developing an effective turnaround plan that makes the company profitable. Additionally, the turnaround practitioner must skillfully carry out the plan. To do so, the practitioner must put into place the tools that will not only save the company in the short term but will also facilitate the company's long-term success. The company's success or failure hinges on these actions.

In rescuing troubled companies, I have observed two realities pertaining to practicing the learned disciplines of management. First, I have yet to go into a troubled company whose management was practicing them in any meaningful degree. Mostly they were not being practiced at all, guaranteeing deficient results. Second, once management began practicing the learned disciplines, it disrupted the spiral of management dysfunction, transforming management effectiveness.

What I observed in these distressed situations was that once management was given the tools to manage effectively, they were able to stage the nucleus of the turnaround. Practicing the learned disciplines of management allowed managers at all levels to make the right things happen and rescue the company, converting unsustainable losses into substantial profits.

To date, I have turned around twenty-eight underperforming and troubled companies. The ability to deploy and practice the learned disciplines of management was integral to this success. The challenge of turning around these companies has provided a radical environment to test and validate the learned disciplines of management effectiveness.

Not unlike automotive engineers who put their prototype vehicles through extreme "torture testing" (in severe Arctic cold and Death Valley heat), which bring to light a vehicle's limitations and inadequacies, turnarounds have tried and tested the learned disciplines of management, proving their reliability.

To use another medical analogy, I imagine that a doctor trained in disease pathology (pathologists examine and analyze diseased organs, tissues, fluids, and whole bodies) has a unique vantage point in seeing firsthand the ravages various diseases have on the human body. A pathologist's work provides a perspective not offered in examining a healthy, disease-free body, and this distinction enables the pathologist to arrive at, construct, and test beneficial treatments.

Likewise, troubled (sick) companies differ from successful (healthy) companies and provide a stark comparison on management practice. In a healthy company, management believes that everything they do is contributing to their success when in fact some activities may not be contributing at all. But in a troubled company, failure teaches you more than success. In a troubled company, you are forced to quickly discover what management practices have led to the company's failure and fix them.

Therefore, turning around troubled companies has provided me a unique and insightful managerial postmortem into management ineffectiveness and failure. Turnarounds have allowed me to examine how a troubled company went on its dismal and destructive path. They have also enabled me to test and validate efficacious solutions, antidotes that the learned disciplines of management provide time and again.

It has been thirty-five years since I was first introduced to the learned disciplines of management. Since then, I have successfully used them to transform management effectiveness in large Fortune 500 public companies and smaller-sized public and private companies in various industries and in diverse departmental specializations throughout the United States, Europe, and Canada.

The industries include beverage operations, building components manufacturing, chemical refinishing, computer manufacturing, construction, consumer and industrial distribution, courier delivery services, electrical and electronic equipment manufacturing, exercise equipment manufacturing, furniture manufacturing, gourmet food purveying, higher education, medical device manufacturing, metal stamping, oil and gas refining, piston ring manufacturing, public utilities, publishing, railroad tank car refurbishing, restaurant operations, retail operations, and steel processing.

The departmental specialties include administration, accounting, customer service, design, engineering, fulfillment, maintenance, manufacturing, marketing, procurement, sales, transportation, and quality assurance.

In the end, I wish to draw no undue attention to my management ability in an unremarkable career. What is important is that the principles contained in this book have been practiced, tested, refined, and validated. Their skillful practice is the secret to your management effectiveness and success. In *The Learned Disciplines of Management,* you will learn how to practice them to make the right things happen.

# Chapter 1

# Planning

If you don't know where you are going, you'll end up someplace else.

— Yogi Berra

The first learned discipline of management is planning, and through its practice, a plan is born. A plan is shaped by an organization's aims and fashioned by the means that obtain the aims. Thus, planning is a twofold discipline based on two determinations: the right aims and the correct means. A plan that effectively integrates these two essential elements is foundational to management successfully making the right things happen.

This twofold planning process is illustrated in one of my favorite movies, the award-winning 1949 film *Twelve O'clock High*, which depicts the operations of an American bomber group based in England during World War II. The movie's story line dramatizes the devastating consequences of having the wrong plan and then shows how the right plan can lead to success.

The movie's opening scenes portray the 918th Heavy Bombardment Group (part of the US Army Eighth Air Force) conducting daylight bombing missions against Nazi Germany. The 918th is commanded by Colonel Davenport.

The missions are going poorly as the 918th suffers heavy losses in both men and bombers. Davenport is overwhelmed as he tries to help his men cope with the stark terror of death — death by German fighters, death by German antiaircraft cannons, and death by a faltering bomber five miles above the earth.

In response to this demand, Colonel Davenport changes his group's planned aims. The new aim is simply to survive the deadly bombing missions. Inevitably, the new aim invites new means. These include launching fewer bombing missions, tolerating pilot excuses for prematurely aborting their bombing runs, ignoring poor performance, justifying poor morale, and depending on luck to make it through a bombing mission alive.

The new plan doesn't help. In fact, things get predictably worse. The 918th's performance becomes unglued as losses mount and the group ceases to be an effective fighting force.

The group's poor performance attracts the attention of its commanding officer, General Pritchard, who launches an investigation into the group's dismal performance. He discovers Colonel Davenport's new plan and, in a pivotal scene, confronts Colonel Davenport, critiquing and condemning the plan. Davenport vehemently defends and justifies it, but Pritchard is unmoved and unconvinced. He has heard enough and relieves Davenport of his command. General Savage, an experienced group commander, is chosen as his replacement.

Savage quickly sizes up the 918th's situation. He recognizes the need for a new plan, one that has the right aims and the correct means for obtaining them. He quickly develops such a plan and presents it to the 918th's aircrews.

He tells the men that the group's aim is to drop bombs on the designated targets. That's it. Period. It is not survival. "Consider yourselves already dead," he declares.

To achieve the new plan's aim, Savage reveals the group's planned means for obtaining it. He directs his crews to fly every bombing mission—he will not tolerate excuses for prematurely turning back. Additionally, each air crewman is expected to perform his duties proficiently: formations will be flown precisely, bombs will be accurately dropped on the designated targets, and the strictest group integrity and discipline will be maintained during an air battle. If a crewmember does not meet these expectations, then appropriate action will be taken against him.

Savage orders his aircrews to commence remedial training to improve their proficiency. They will practice the fundamentals until they become second nature. Finally, General Savage stresses that skill, not luck, will make the group effective and better their chances of surviving.

Savage's plan marks a new beginning for the 918th. It focuses the group on the right aims and the correct means for achieving them. In a short time, the 918th is transformed into a proficient bomber group, one that drops bombs on the designated targets.[1]

Note the plan's aim. It gave the right answer to the question, what is the group's aim? The right answer was to drop bombs on the targets. For a bomber group in war, it does not get any more succinct.

Note too that the planned means flowed out of the plan's aim. The means required aircrews to develop, through constant training, the necessary skills to drop bombs on the targets. The right plan was transformative; empowering the 918th to successfully achieve its purpose.

Although this is a fictional story (based on a real general and events) about a bomber group during World War II, real-life examples abound that directly relate to management not rightly practicing the twofold planning discipline essential for success.

Yogi Berra said, "If you don't know where you are going, you'll end up someplace else."[2] When planning is not practiced effectively, organizations inevitably end up someplace else, and that place is rarely where they wanted to be.

## Planning's Essential Elements

Effective planning must answer two vital questions: What are the organization's aims, and what are the means for achieving them?

A plan is a tool much like a construction blueprint. A blueprint depicts the project's aims and specifies the best means to obtain them. Likewise, effective planning combines the right aims and the appropriate means. These elements make a plan executable; guiding, informing, and directing management to a successful outcome.

Unfortunately, what passes for planning in many organizations is simply a perfunctory exercise lacking any practical significance. It results in plans that read more like children's fairytales than blueprints. In these organizations, planning is not seen as a dynamic juggernaut that animates an entire organization but as an obligatory formality. These plans are not road maps that galvanize action but stories that stifle performance.

However, in addition to vague plans are wrong plans—plans that fail to arrive at the right aims and correct means for achieving the aims. Collectively, these ineffective plans contribute to management's inability to make the right things happen. Thus, effective planning must incorporate several essential elements that include establishing the right aims, determining the right means, and making the aims and means specific and measurable.

## The Wrong Aims

Financially troubled companies often arrive at the wrong planned aims (I'll discuss the wrong means later in this chapter). This happens as management struggles to survive. When their plan fails, they try another. As they enact these changes in plans, compromises are made, and each plan becomes weaker, demanding less than the one before it. This process further deteriorates management effectiveness and the organization's performance, further imperiling the company's future.

Although the company's initial planned aim was to make a suitable profit, by the time I arrive to turn around the company, its aim has changed. Often the aim is watered down; focused simply on survival. For example, to breakeven or not lose as much money as the year before. These tentative plans are half measures that only make matters worse, further jeopardizing the company.

An example where management chose the wrong aims is illustrated when Rich Wagoner took over as CEO of General Motors in 2000. Wagoner set a bold plan to increase the company's market share, which had fallen two-thirds from a 1960 peak.

In Wagoner's defense, market share had been the historic measure of success in the auto industry. For instance, auto companies such as Toyota and Honda had thrived through growing their share of the North American market.

But as it turned out, Wagoner's plan failed to take into account several significant changes. First, foreign rivals had several competitive advantages over GM such as shorter new model development times and a lack of legacy pension and health care costs. Second, GM itself had changed over the years. It had allowed its costs, particularly its labor costs and debt to spiral out of control. Thus, GM was severely limited in its operational choices and global competiveness.

GM's focus on increasing market share caused profit margins to decline. Nine months into 2005, GM was in serious trouble, having lost nearly $5 billion, as it continued to prop up North American sales and market share through heavy discounts.

Fast-forward to 2008, when GM announced it had lost $39 billion in twelve months. In that same year, Wagoner announced a new plan aim that was "a blueprint for creating a new General Motors, one that is lean, profitable, self-sustaining and fully committed to product excellence and technology leadership."[3]

But it was too late for a seemingly right plan aim. By 2009, the company was bankrupt. One can only surmise what might have been had Wagoner and GM chosen in 2000 the seemingly right plan aims that were announced eight years later.

## The Right Aims

Effective planning requires management to establish the organization's right aims. This is management's only recourse, for until an organization is mobilized toward the right aims, its efforts are misdirected and it resources squandered.

The importance of establishing the right plan aims was underscored while I was turning around a metal fastener manufacturer. The company had not made a profit in eight years. In the last twelve months, it had lost $400,000 on $3.5 million in sales. The continued losses caused the company's management to go into survival mode as they further watered down the organization's aims hoping not to lose as much money as the year before.

The company's owner had rejected this mediocre profit aim. He was no longer willing to fund shoddy results and had decided to close the plant and liquidate its assets—that is, until I persuaded him to try and turn the company around. Managing the company was now my responsibility.

The first thing I did was establish a new plan aim, one that would cause management to pursue excellence instead of mediocre results. I researched what these excellent results might be among the best-performing companies in the industry. The data among this group indicated that earning 8 percent on sales was achievable. So this became the new plan aim. Specifically and measurably, this 8 percent meant obtaining $280,000 in profits on $3.5 million in sales.

Some thought this was an unrealistic, even foolhardy, aim, given the company's profitless history. These were the same executives who thought the company could not be turned around and should be liquidated, the same executives who had acquiesced to the company's wrong aims over an eight-year period.

But we ignored our critics and pressed on with a planned aim of earning an 8 percent profit. The new aim now caused us to determine the means that would produce a $280,000 profit. The new means meant finding ways to reduce operating expenses by $680,000 ($280,000 in profits plus $400,000 in previous losses).

The new means impacted how the business operated, including how materials were purchased, products priced, equipment scheduled, employees managed, and other expenses incurred. In other words, the new aim focused the entire organization on pursuing excellent results instead of mediocre ones, dictating how every dollar was spent.

The new plan aim had a galvanizing effect on the management team. Up until now, management had pursued mediocre aims while achieving inferior results. Understandably, pursuing mediocrity is not very motivating. Now that the organization's aims were set on obtaining excellent results, the company's management team eagerly began pursing them.

These are several examples that resulted from the new plan. In total, the company had spent $680,000 more in the previous year than its best-performing competitors. We began to look at the possibility that the company had overspent on its major purchases. To ensure against this possibility, we solicited multiple bids from various vendors for the major items the company purchased.

The company's biggest purchase expense was steel. As we solicited the best steel prices, we asked the company's steel suppliers to give us their best price. We stressed that we were no longer interested in the perks they had showered on the company's previous executives, such as free tickets, trips, and other gifts. Soliciting better steel pricing paid off as we reduced annual steel purchases $250,000.

Next, we made sure the company's spending was prudent and necessary. If the expenditure did not support keeping the business operating, it was eliminated. Using this bare standard, we were able to slash another $120,000 in miscellaneous expenses from the company's budget.

For example, the company was paying a landscape service $300 per month to maintain the company's grounds. This expenditure was deemed unacceptable in light of the new plan aim. We canceled the service and asked one of the maintenance men to tend to the grounds during his infrequent downtime. Admittedly, the grounds did not look as good as when the company had a professional service keeping them, but having well-manicured grounds was not the aim.

Finally, we gave the company's managers the means to manage resources and results more effectively. Quickly, the learned disciplines of management were developed, designed, and deployed throughout the company. Once deployed, managers began using them to make the right things happen. These right things increased employee productivity.

For example, productivity improvements allowed us to eliminate twelve manufacturing positions and stop using overtime. Managing more effectively allowed the company to optimize resources and maximize results, reducing expenses another $330,000.

Our new aim produced stunning results. The company made a $300,000 annual profit (exceeding the $280,000 planned profit aim), the first in nine years and a profit level comparable to the best-performing companies in the industry.

## Specific and Measurable Aims

Not only must the plan's aims be the right ones, but they also must be specific and measurable (I'll discuss specific and measurable means later in this chapter).

Specificity requires that management rigorously arrive at the aim's precise details. Lack of specifics is one reason an organization does make progress in achieving its aims. Vague aims render a plan immeasurable, thus making it impracticable to manage. As will be discussed in chapter 3, "Measuring Performance," measurability promotes manageability and is a critical consideration in arriving at a plan's aims (and means).

An example of a poorly executed plan, where the organization's aims were not specified, occurred at a Midwestern conglomerate doing approximately $100 million in sales. My firm was engaged to turn around one of the conglomerate's five companies, but while this effort was taking place, I became entangled in how the entire conglomerate's planning process took place.

The conglomerate's planning process occurred in the year's final quarter, took six weeks' time, and involved every manager in the company. It began with the conglomerate's CFO asking each department manager to put together a departmental budget for the coming year.

Over the past five years, this planning process had produced less than stellar results; profits were barely above breakeven. The CEO and the company's stockholders stated this financial performance was unacceptable. They suggested that the company's managers plan for a more "significant" profit in the coming year.

I asked the CFO what "significant" profit meant, and he answered that it would have to be much better than the past few years. He was hoping the managers would plan for at least a 3 percent profit. But he did not tell them what to plan for, secretly hoping it might be more.

There was considerable anticipation surrounding the conclusion of the planning process. This was when each department's plan (including projected sales and budgeted expenses) was presented to the conglomerate's executive committee. The committee scrutinized these plans, while the department's managers defended them. At the session's close, the plans were approved. The plans were then tabulated and represented the entire conglomerate's planned profit aim for the upcoming year.

The results were anticlimactic.

Management had planned a paltry (for a $100 million company) $600,000 profit. This planned profit shocked and disappointed the company's CEO and shareholders. The new plan's profit aim was less than 1 percent of sales. It was the lowest planned profit aim management had made in five years, and it was much less than the 3 percent profit the executive committee was secretly hoping for.

Although the conglomerate's planning process was not my concern, I could not resist commenting on it. Shortly after the results had been announced, I met with the CEO to update him on our consulting project's progress. During the meeting, I shared my observations and criticisms about the way the company went about its planning process. And I poked fun at the meager results.

Understandably, the CEO was not in a good-humored mood. He took umbrage at my comments and declared, "Show me the money!" As we talked further, I realized he was not joking. He told me to postpone my current consulting work and to advise him and his management team on how to conduct an effective planning process. At the end of the meeting, he reinforced his expectations, exclaiming once again, "You show me the money!"

In evaluating the conglomerate's planning process, I noted that making a significant profit was certainly the right aim. But, specifically, what should the plan's profit aim be?

I observed that the CFO and the other executive committee members never answered this question. They had not given their managers a specific and measureable aim. I was determined not to fall into the same trap as I began advising management in how to develop an effective plan.

By researching the conglomerate's various industries and their respective business ratios, I arrived at several profit outcomes for a comparable group of companies doing $100 million in sales. The poorest-performing ones made a $400,000 profit (0.04 percent on sales), the median group made a $1.4 million profit (1.4 percent on sales), while the best-performing group made a $3.8 million profit (3.8 percent on sales).

With this data at the ready, I met with the CEO. I pointed out that his current planning process was flawed because it did not establish a specific and thus measurable aim. Instead, his management team relied on a subjective, trickle-down planning process to arrive at the plan's aims. This approach allowed his managers to choose an easy route in establishing their departmental aims. Predictably, easy routes produce mediocre results. For proof, we had to look no further than the less than 1 percent profit aim his management team's plans proposed.

I suggested that the planning process begin with an aim that was both specific and measurable. This made the plan executable, providing the necessary direction to each department manager in arriving at the appropriate means to achieve the planned aims.

Based on my research, I laid out three such profit aims: 0.04, 1.4, and 3.8 percent. Now, it was the CEO's decision to choose which specific and measurable profit aim the organization should pursue. He chose 3.8 percent.

The conglomerate's planning process was extended for another week; only this time, management began with a specific and measurable aim. The CEO asked his department managers to develop a plan whose means would obtain a 3.8 percent profit.

During the week, I met with each manager to facilitate his or her planning. In the meetings, I discovered the new aim had a decided impact on the company's managers and could be best described as comical dysfunction.

Over the years, management had grown accustomed to a flawed planning process—one that had low expectations and little accountability. For many managers, having a specific and measureable planned aim was intimidating and overwhelming. Initially, they tried to ignore the new aim, hoping the CEO would revert back to his old ways. But they quickly abandoned this approach when the CEO told them, in no uncertain terms, "Show me the money!" It was only then that they begrudgingly acceded to the new aim—but not wholeheartedly.

One manager whom we'll call Ted quickly responded to the new planning process. He put together a perfunctory budget that produced a 4 percent profit. I told Ted that his budget results would be reviewed monthly against the plan's aim. If his actual sales and expenses were not in-line with his planned profits, he would have to take the appropriate action to remedy the situation.

Ted's face turned pale. He stammered in disbelief, "We have always reviewed our plans at year end. Not every month. If we missed our numbers, we would try harder the next year."

"That may be how you operated before, but not now," I replied. "Now your results will be measured each month, and if your results are not what they should be, you'll be expected to do something about it right away, not when the year is over and it's too late."

After our meeting, Ted prepared a new budget. The one he resubmitted to the executive committee hardly resembled the two earlier ones he had presented. But this time it realistically spelled out the means to reach a 3.8 percent profit aim.

The most typical response to the new plan's aim was one taken by a manager we'll call Andrew.

In our meeting, he stubbornly declared, "What the executives around here are asking for cannot be done." Pointing to the

CEO's memo on his desk he said: "If I tried to meet their imposed profit levels, I would have to reduce our projected sales by $100,000. In my earlier budget, I was only trying to be optimistic. But if the CEO is really going to expect me to hit a 4 percent profit level, then I can't afford to be optimistic. In today's market conditions, we'll have a tough time holding onto the sales we have, let alone increasing them." Shaking his head and in a dismissive tone he continued: "Without planned sales growth, I'll have to ransack my department through aggressive cost cutting. For instance, I'll have to eliminate the new equipment purchases I was counting on and I'll have to lay off three repair technicians. Is the CEO aware of the consequences his rash edict will cause?"

I replied that Andrew would have the chance to tell the CEO himself when he presented his new plan to the executive committee.

It turned out that "ransacking" the department through aggressive cost cutting meant canceling equipment purchases that were on Andrew's "wish list" but did not impair the ongoing operations of the department. It also meant firing three repair technicians who were hired three years before based on projected sales growth that never materialized.

As the extended planning session came to a close, the various plans were tabulated and we had a much different result to show the CEO. Having a specific and measurable planned aim allowed us to "show him the money." The conglomerate's new planned profit aim was $3.5 million (albeit on lowered projected sales). This was almost $3 million more in profits than the desultory $600,000 management had planned for only the week before. "Show me the money" indeed!

## The Wrong Means

An effective plan must also arrive at the correct means for achieving the organization's aims. Although deciding on the right planned aim is a critical first step, it does not always lead to determining the correct means. You would think that getting the aim right would automatically lead to arriving at the correct means, but this is not always the case. It is possible to have a plan that couples the incorrect means to right aims. This is unfortunate because the wrong means will not achieve the organization's aims.

For example, a company that designed and produced interior decorating accessories retained my firm. Despite management's best efforts, this company's performance and profitability were in steep decline. Among the company's far-flung operations was an intercity call center that epitomized poor performance and was a constant drain on profits.

The call center employed hundreds of customer service representatives. Their job was to take customers' orders and provide other customer sales support. Over the years, management struggled to get this vital and costly center to perform, to effectively and efficiently meet customers' needs.

Unceasing customer complaints marked this struggle. Customers complained of long wait times, which the call center's internally generated measures confirmed. These measures indicated that during peak calling hours, the customer had to wait, on average, fourteen minutes before a representative answered the call.

Customers also complained about the call center's poor service. This was reflected in frequently conducted customer surveys where the call center's service was rated poor or very poor—the worst possible ratings out of five possible choices (excellent, above average, average, poor, and very poor).

In response to these complaints, management decided a new means was needed to achieve its aim of providing excellent service to customers. Management believed that the means had to address what they saw as the problem's source: that the customer service representatives were not motivated to serve the customer. They saw lacking motivation as the reason why customer calls were not answered quickly enough and why customer concerns were not addressed sufficiently.

In an effort to solve the problem through a more effective means, management decided to ask each employee to get on the phone and stay on the phone until the customer's needs were met. To ensure that this new means was carried out, each employee's time spent on the phone was measured. This measure would establish how well each employee performed the new means.

For example, if a representative was on the phone for 360 minutes during a 480-minute (eight-hour) shift, the representative's performance was measured at 75 percent (360÷480). If a representative was on the phone for 48 minutes during a 480-minute shift, the representative's performance was measured at only 10 percent (48÷480).

But was this the right means? The performance results told the answer. The new means had been in effect for twelve months, and over that time, the call center's performance results had not improved but had inexplicably grown worse.

The new plan's means had been successful in one respect — the customer service representatives were on the phone more — much more. Their average call duration increased from three to five minutes, causing already long customer wait times to soar.

Despite being on the phone longer, customers were still not pleased. In customer surveys, the service experience continued to be rated as poor or very poor. This feedback and the increasing workload increased pressure on management to hire more employees and have the existing employees work more overtime. Meanwhile, management had no clear alternative means to address the growing work volume and expenses amid increasingly lousy results.

What went wrong? Management had arrived at the wrong means to achieve their aims.

Management's failure, in a misguided effort to derive the correct means, implemented the wrong means that produced unintended consequences. The new means did not achieve the organization's aim, but instead made the situation worse—much worse.

How the new means proved to be the wrong means became obvious as I observed the new means in action. The new means asked employees to get on the phone and stay on the phone with their performance being measured accordingly. So that is exactly what they did. What should have been a two minute phone conversation grew into a five or even a ten minute one. Since employee performance was measured on how much time they spent on the phone, they tried to stay on the phone as long as possible.

They did this by engaging the customer in conversation, talking about the weather, family life, and other familiar topics to stretch the conversation out as long as possible. They took every opportunity to place the customer on hold so they could go on an "information search." While the customer was on hold, they ran errands and chatted with co-workers as their minute total grew and the customer stewed or hung up. Under these circumstances, it became even more difficult for a customer to place an order quickly or to have issues promptly resolved. These were not the results management had in mind when they chose the means they did.

## The Right Means

Management's misguided means did not work because management had wrongly assumed that spending more time on the phone meant calls would be answered more quickly and customer's requests would appropriately be addressed. As the results demonstrated, the basis for the means turned out to be irrelevant and counterproductive.

To achieve the call center's aims, the correct means had to be found. This was accomplished through practicing the learned disciplines of management.

For example, performance was measured using a performance standard derived for each call center activity. Then the employee's actual performance was measured and compared to this ideal standard.

For instance, if processing an order should take three minutes, this was the performance expected. By settling on the correct means, management was able to use it to obtain the organization's aim of providing excellent, low-cost customer service.

Evidence that management had arrived at the right means was seen when peak wait times plummeted from fourteen minutes to five minutes. The average call duration declined from five minutes to two minutes. And, for the first time, surveyed customers responses were positive. Customers rated their call center experience as above average or excellent.

A surveyed customer provided my favorite response. She asked, "When did you guys outsource your call center?" Although this customer was unknowingly asking about the call center she had always used, it was not the same. It had been transformed through management determining the correct means to achieve the plan's aim.

## Specific and Measurable Means

We have already discussed the importance of making the plan's aims specific and measurable. In the same way, the plan's *means* must also be specific and measurable to make them manageable.

An example of making the means specific and measurable

occurred at a large industrial sales company my firm consulted. The company's planned aim called for 10 percent sales growth while maintaining current profit margins.

To achieve this, management had selected the means. They asked their salespeople to make more targeted sales calls on existing customers and make more sales calls on new customers. When this new planned means went into effect, nothing happened; there was no increase in sales. This was when my client asked me to identify why the means were not achieving the aim and to offer a remedy.

My first step was to observe the salespeople carrying out the new means. As I did so, the problem became clear. The plan's means were not specific and therefore not measurable. Consequently, without specificity, the salespeople's normal routine was not impacted, and they never got around to making their assigned sales calls. And without measurability, managing the salespeople's performance was rendered ineffectual.

To address the situation, we developed a specific and measurable means to achieve the plan's aims. This entailed giving each salesperson a weekly assignment of calling on five actual existing customers who had targeted (identified products the customer was not purchasing) sales potential. Additionally, they were assigned five specific potential customers to call on. The ten weekly assignments were measured on whether they were completed, and the salespeople were followed up on weekly for compliance.

This new means disrupted the status quo and allowed for more effective management, producing immediate results of increased sales to both existing and new customers.

## Conclusion

In the equation for management effectiveness, an organization's plan is the fixed integer on the left side of the equal sign, and all that management does is on the right. An effective plan lays the foundation for management success as it rightly establishes the organization's aims and correctly determines the means for achieving them, rendering both specific and measureable.

Although planning stands alone in our equation, achieving the plan requires practicing six other management disciplines. The first of these, the discipline of organizing, is our next stop.

## Chapter 2

# Organizing

Many things which cannot be overcome when they are together yield themselves up when taken little by little.

—Plutarch

For want of a nail the shoe was lost.
For want of a shoe the horse was lost.
For want of a horse the rider was lost.
For want of a rider the battle was lost.
For want of a battle the kingdom was lost.
And all for the want of a horseshoe nail.

—English proverb

This old English proverb dramatizes an essential connection: the indelible link between an organization's aims and the resources required for achieving them. Neglecting this linkage is costly.

Organizing is an antidote for this neglect. Through its practice, the crucial connection between an organization's aims and the resources necessary to achieve them is reinforced. Organizing does this in two ways. First, it makes certain that the required resources are available so that essential activities can be performed successfully. Second, activities are organized to ensure they use resources efficiently and effectively. When these two organizing aspects are carried out, the result is resources and results being maximized, which contributes to management making the right things happen.

Organizing is a time-consuming, deliberate, and exacting process. Its jumping-off point is to recognize all the activities that must be performed to achieve the organization's aims. Once identified, these activities must be thoroughly understood. It is only after the activities have been identified and understood that management can evaluate whether the activities maximize resources and results. If it is determined that they do not, management acts to optimally organize them.

Carrying out these dictates can seem overwhelming at first. Fortunately, this process is best approached little by little, making it manageable. As Plutarch, an ancient Greek historian, rightly observed, "Many things which cannot be overcome when they are together, yield themselves up when taken little by little."[1] As we shall see, this painstaking approach to organizing pays huge dividends.

## Recognize the Activities

An organization's goals are achieved through its established means. These means, made up of various activities, must be performed successfully. Therefore, it is incumbent that management not only recognize what these activities are but to break the activities down to identify the various steps, processes, procedures, and resources that are required to successfully complete the activities.

This process of recognizing activities and identifying their various elements is crucial. It results in management thoroughly understanding the activity. This knowledge then enables management to effectively evaluate whether the activity is optimally organized. Before the activities can be thoroughly understood and evaluated, they first must be recognized.

For example, if the organization's aim is to grow sales by 10 percent, then performing more sales calls would be an recognized activity. If the organization's aim is to eliminate trade receivables over sixty days, then making phone calls on delinquent accounts would be an recognized activity. Each activity has various components that must be identified. For example, performing more sales calls entails selecting prospective customers, setting and carrying out sales call appointments, making sales proposals, processing customer orders and determining if a salesperson has additional time available to perform these steps.

Often, recognizing the organization's activities is a straightforward process. However, some situations make the process challenging.

For example, a jet engine turbine fan manufacturer was losing money but did not know why. Management had assumed they had recognized all the activities (and their respective costs) that went into manufacturing a turbine fan. Based on this assumption, they arrived at a seemingly profitable product price. But as it turned out, the price was too low, causing financial losses to mount. Baffled, the company's management turned to our consulting firm for help.

Our consultants' approach to solving the riddle was to methodically practice the learned disciplines of management. Through the discipline of organizing, we recognized all the company's manufacturing activities. These activities were further broken down into their individual processes and evaluated as to whether they reflected the established manufacturing cost. This effort to recognize all the activities brought to the surface the source of the company's losses. The management was shocked to discover they had overlooked an activity, one that stood out glaringly on the comprehensive activity list the consultants prepared.

Although management had recognized all the turbine fan manufacturing activities when everything was going smoothly, they had missed an activity when the manufacturing process went awry. Unbeknownst to management, a significant number of turbine blades were being reworked or scrapped because they were out of tolerance. This happened as machine operators spotted deficient parts and took the initiative (without notifying management) to send them back up the line to be reworked or to be scrapped by the machine operators who made them.

Without being informed otherwise, management had assumed the manufacturing activities were going smoothly. Consequently, this inaccurate assumption led to understated manufacturing costs and a selling price that was too low to make a profit. This oversight explained why the company was losing money.

Once *all* the activities were recognized, management used this information to accomplish its aims. For example, management reengineered the manufacturing processes, resulting in a dramatic reduction in out-of-tolerance parts. The cost to rework or scrap the remaining out-of-tolerance parts was built into the new selling price. With these changes, the company quickly became profitable.

Another challenging situation is to recognize an activity that is not being performed but should be. Because the activity is not being done, it cannot be observed, thus making it difficult to recognize. Fortunately, the activity not being done produces consequences that can be observed, making recognizing the activity possible.

This situation arose for a failing consumer products manufacturer. The company had many problems, but its most alarming and mystifying problem was its reported product quality. One wholesale customer provided quality feedback as they tracked the weekly number of defective units their customers had returned. They reported the manufacturer's failure rate at a whopping 25 percent. The wholesaler stated that if the product quality did not quickly improve, they would cancel their purchase contract.

The reported quality problem was a special mystery because each unit was stringently tested using state-of-the-art testing equipment before it left the plant. This testing took place on each of the plant's nine manufacturing lines, where assembled units were conveyed to a quality test technician. The technician attached the unit to the test equipment where it was "burned in" and its components tested. Only those units that passed were shipped to the customer. The units that did not pass were tagged and sent back up the line to be torn apart, reassembled, and tested again.

The company's managers were stumped. What could be causing such a discrepancy in the testing results and the customer's experience? In an attempt to answer this question, we asked to meet with the testing equipment manufacturer's representative. The company sent an engineer who provided the first break in the unfolding mystery.

We explained the situation to the engineer and asked if the testing equipment could be the source of the quality problem. The engineer asked to see the equipment. The maintenance staff along with the management team led the engineer out onto the shop floor to where the test equipment was located.

The first question the engineer asked the maintenance staff was how often they recalibrated the test machines (a process that was specified in the equipment manual to take place every thirty days). Puzzled and pained expressions formed on their faces as they tried to remember the last time they had done so. They sheepishly acknowledged that it had been awhile — maybe six months ago, maybe longer. They really could not remember when they last did it.

Shortly after our meeting ended, the maintenance staff recalibrated the test equipment. It turned out that the test equipment on eight production lines was functioning within their performance specifications. However, the test equipment on line nine, the highest-volume line, turned out to not be functioning at all. Although the control panel indicated a positive test result, this was misleading, for the test equipment was not actually working.

This situation was made worse because no units were being returned to the assemblers. As a result, their work got sloppier as they concluded that making a concentrated effort to assemble a quality unit was not necessary. Line nine, with its defective test equipment, was the source of our quality problem. Through this fiasco, we recognized a crucial activity that was not being performed: recalibrating the testing equipment monthly.

Two other situations make activity recognition challenging. The first situation is where an activity has been recognized but it is the wrong activity and shouldn't be performed. The second situation is recognizing an activity that should be performed but does not exist.

An example in which the wrong activity is recognized occurred while I was organizing a large public utility's purchasing department. To begin, I set about recognizing the various activities the department performed.

An activity cropped up and was added to my growing list: "Track down purchase order specifications." I asked the manager, "Why do you have to track down this information? I would think all the information you needed was provided on the purchase order request."

"Most departments do a good job giving us the information we need, but not construction," he replied. "Construction managers are notorious for submitting incomplete or confusing purchase order requests. When this happens, we have to track down the needed information to process the purchase order."

Further research indicated that one out of every three construction purchase order requests lacked the necessary information. Because the construction department originated most purchase order requests, tracking down this information added significantly to the purchasing department's workload (and indirectly to the construction department's workload because their fieldwork was often interrupted by calls from purchasing seeking the missing information amid the noise of a busy construction site).

Tracking down purchase order specifications was an activity the purchasing staff had been doing for years, and it was understandable that they recognized it as an activity they performed. But this activity caused the wrong things to happen: wasting employees' time and delaying the purchase of necessary materials.

All of this raised the question, could this activity be avoided entirely? Although tracking down information had initially showed up on the list of recognized activities, after some consideration, it was decided that it shouldn't be done and was taken off the list.

To prevent this activity from being necessary, the submittal of incomplete purchase orders had to be addressed. It was a simple fix: we established a policy of not accepting incomplete purchase orders. If a submitted purchase order request was incomplete, it was stamped "INCOMPLETE SPECIFICATIONS" and summarily returned to its originator. Tracking down purchase order specifications was not a legitimate activity and was not recognized as an activity purchasing should perform. Similarly, a preventable activity that wastes resources and squanders results should not be recognized as a legitimate activity but appropriately dealt with.

Now let's talk about the challenge of recognizing an activity that does not exist but should. For example, I was helping a client organize a customer service department. While observing and recognizing the various activities the department performed (including taking customers' orders), I was shocked at the number of items that were out of stock.

I was shocked because the frequent stock-outs were contrary to an accounting report I had read. The report cited that stock-out items occurred less than 1 percent of the time. This meant that the purchasing department was doing a good job controlling inventory, but that is not what I had observed.

The customer service representatives' actions explained the disparity. The representatives were skilled at avoiding lost sales due to stock-outs. When this situation arose, they tried to persuade the customers to substitute their ordered item for a similar, in-stock item. These substituted items were not the customer's first choice; in many cases, the customer acquiesced to the change out of necessity. It was only when a customer did not or could not agree to a substitution that a stock-out was recorded. Accounting had accurately measured this occurrence at less than 1 percent of the time. But this measure did not tell the whole story, thus giving management a false estimation of purchasing's effectiveness.

To accurately measure the actual number of stock-outs, I recognized an activity that did not yet exist. This newly created activity asked customer service representatives to document when a stock-out occurred, regardless of whether a sale was lost.

Once implemented, this activity revealed that stock-outs were happening far more than previously reported. In fact, the actual stock-out rate was 7 percent. In addition to recording how often stock-outs occurred, the new procedure also documented the items that were out of stock and, when a substitution occurred, what item was substituted.

This feedback was given to the purchasing department so that they could better control what inventory to keep on hand and correct the customer's order history. Correcting the customer's order history was necessary because purchasing agents were now stocking substituted items rather than the ones the customer originally ordered. Without this corrective feedback, the company would only perpetuate stock-outs, frustrating customers' order preferences and adding to the customer service representatives' workload as they juggled to substitute frequently occurring stocked-out items.

As these examples illustrate, there is a decisive litmus test in recognizing the activities that achieve the organization's aims. It answers the question, have all the activities (and their individual parts) been recognized? These activities should be nothing more, nothing less, and nothing else.

## Understand the Activity

Once all the activities have been recognized, management then strives to thoroughly understand them. This important second step includes discovering why activities need to be performed, identifying who performs the activities, observing how the activities are performed and when, and determining what resources are necessary to successfully complete the activities. Answering these questions is important because it prepares management for evaluating whether the activity is optimally organized. It also enables management to take appropriate action if the activity is not optimally organized.

An example of thoroughly understanding an activity took place at a company that made exercise equipment. This failing company had a reputation for innovative products that contributed to its growing sales. However, the company struggled to profitably produce its products and hired me to turn around their manufacturing operations. The company's manufacturing operations consisted of six different departments, each having their own problems. But there was one problem all the departments shared: a parts shortage. And this problem had one source, the plant's Metal Cutting Department. I began my turnaround efforts there.

The Metal Cutting Department was responsible for cutting the tubular and solid steel parts that went into every exercise equipment model. Unfortunately, the department could not supply enough parts for the plant's growing production demands. Management concluded that the department's problem was insufficient manufacturing capacity. To solve this perceived problem, management had approved the purchase of another computer-controlled (CC) saw (installed cost $80,000). Since optimally organizing the department was already one of my stated aims, the plant's management asked me to confirm whether one additional metal cutting saw would be enough or would more be needed.

To begin practicing organizing, I embedded myself in the

Metal Cutting Department. A typical workday was spent simply watching the department's activities being performed while gathering much-needed information. The first information I needed was to recognize all the department's activities. Next, I had to thoroughly understand them. That meant identifying each step, process, and method an employee used to cut metal parts, including indentifying and measuring the resources these required. Obtaining this information would allow me to evaluate how well the activity was organized and enable me to optimally organize it if need be.

Fortunately, the metal cutting activities were uncomplicated, making their identification uneventful. However, the result of thoroughly understanding the identified activities was anything but uneventful. For this knowledge shook management's presumptions and transformed how the department was organized and performed.

Thoroughly understanding the department's activities came about as I eagerly began observing them (stopwatch in hand to measure how efficiently resources were used). I anticipated seeing these large, powerful saws quickly cutting through thick bundles of steel. Before the shift began, I was informed that two departments had run out of cut metal parts and had to be shut down. So acute was this problem that the plant manager was contemplating closing the rest of the plant until the Metal Cutting Department could catch up in supplying the needed parts.

Given this dire situation, I was expecting to see the department's employees urgently cutting steel parts. At the time, however, I didn't realize how long I'd have to wait to see this activity actually being performed. The saws would not begin working for several more hours.

The department had one high-capacity CC saw (plus an assortment of infrequently used specialty metal cutting saws). It was this CC saw that supplied most of the plant's parts, and I concentrated on understanding how this activity was carried out.

A buzzer sounded signaling the shift's start. The employee who operated the CC saw was given a daily production schedule that listed the type and quantity of the various exercise equipment models scheduled to be manufactured. It was difficult for the saw operator to read the production schedule in the dimly lit plant. Nevertheless, he reached for a tattered and smudged notebook that broke down each model's cut parts. Using the notebook, a pencil, paper, and a handheld calculator, the operator slowly began calculating how many different kinds of parts he had to cut. When this was finished, he put together a list of the particular steel that was required. With this information, the operator compiled a CC saw cutting schedule, one that attempted to combine similar cuts so as to limit the time-consuming saw setups he'd have to make.

It took the saw operator about an hour to complete these deliberations. Meanwhile, the saw sat idle (along with a third of the plant). With his penciled list in hand, the operator searched for the steel bundles he planned to cut and gathered them on steel on carts. The carts were then staged for when they would be wheeled into the saw's feeding area.

Next, the operator changed the saw blade that had grown dull during the previous shift. Then, finally, he began cutting metal parts—two hours after the shift had begun. But the cutting did not go on for long before the mid-morning buzzer sounded, signaling a fifteen-minute break. The CC saw operator trudged off to join the other plant employees for coffee. It was mid-morning; the CC saw sat idle once again. Meanwhile, no parts had yet been delivered to the other departments.

After the break, the operator resumed his cutting. Soon, the first scheduled parts were finished. He turned the saw off, restacked the cut metal parts, and carted them off to the waiting departments. This process of cutting, stacking, and delivering parts went on for the rest of the morning until the buzzer sounded again signaling the plant's half-hour lunch break. I was told that another department had run out of parts as the

CC saw sat quietly.

After lunch, the part's cutting, restacking, and delivering resumed. This was interrupted when another buzzer announced the afternoon break. Work resumed until the buzzer sounded once more, signaling the workday's end.

I added up the time the CC saw had actually been used. The total was only two hours and thirty-two minutes over an eight-hour shift. For the next four days, I continued to observe (and measure) the CC saw, seeking to thoroughly understand this vital activity. Shockingly, the CC saw never ran for more than three hours during an eight-hour shift. During one shift, it ran for only one hour and forty-five minutes. Observing, studying, and measuring this activity deepened my understanding of it. This understanding allowed me to evaluate how well the activity was organized and (when I concluded that the activity was poorly organized) to facilitate optimally organizing it.

For example, optimal organizing meant the CC saw would be fully used. To facilitate this, we made several changes. First, we changed how the saw operator planned cutting metal parts. Instead of having the saw operator do it, an office employee (using a computer spreadsheet) did the task. Second, another employee staged the steel for the CC saw operator and also stacked and delivered the cut parts. The maintenance staff changed the dull blade before the shift began. Operator breaks were staggered, allowing the saws to run throughout the shift.

When these activities were reorganized, the CC saw seldom stopped running. Its utilization skyrocketed to over 90 percent (up from 25 percent), resulting in the plant's other departments getting the cut parts they needed. The order for a second CC metal cutting saw was canceled. Thoroughly understanding an activity facilitated it being optimally organized. This in turn impacted the plant's productivity, enabling the company to make a profit—something it had not been able to do for five years.

## Evaluating Organization

Once all the activities have been recognized and their various processes identified and thoroughly understood, what do you do with them? You evaluate whether they are optimally organized. Evaluating how well an activity is organized guarantees that resources are ordered and coordinated so that the activity can be successfully performed and ensures that employed resources are used effectively and efficiently.

In evaluating how well an activity is organized, it is helpful to simply ask *why* an activity is organized and performed the way it is. For instance, *why* isn't the activity done smarter, faster, better, and cheaper?

The automaker Toyota is known for its efficiently produced, high-quality automobiles. The company's success is attributed to its organizing philosophy known as the Toyota Production System. The system's central tenant is to ask why activities are organized and performed the way they are. To quote former Toyota executive vice president Taiichi Ohno, "Observe the production floor without preconceptions and with a blank mind. Repeat 'why' five times about every matter."[2]

Asking "why" not only aids management in evaluating how an activity is organized and performed but also how it *should* be organized and performed.

An activity that is optimally organized maximizes results and resources. Conversely, a poorly organized activity diminishes results and resources. Thus a poorly organized activity uses more resources while producing fewer results, whereas a well-organized activity uses fewer resources while producing more results. For example, we see this in how cars are evaluated. A car that goes forty miles on a gallon of gasoline is said to get good gas mileage (maximizes resources), whereas a car that goes seven miles on a gallon of gasoline is said to get poor gas mileage (minimizes resources).

Maximizing resources (people, equipment, materials, supplies, etc.) is what effective management does. Thus, individual activities (and the interaction between integrated activities) are analyzed and evaluated to determine how effectively and efficiently they use resources.

The discipline of organizing focuses on both the effective and efficient use of resources. For it is possible to use resources efficiently but to fail to effectively accomplish the activity's intended results. It is also possible for an activity to effectively accomplish its intended results but to do so inefficiently, wasting resources in the process.

Evaluating how optimally an activity is organized requires measuring how it is performed. One way to do this is to measure how *effectively* an activity is performed. For instance, salespeople's effectiveness is measured by the number of sales orders they generate compared to the number of sales calls they make. If a salesperson makes 20 sales calls resulting in 5 sales orders, that salesperson's measured effectiveness is 25 percent (5 ÷ 20).

Or take measuring a process's effectiveness. Say a process produced 100 units of which 8 units were defective and 92 units were faultless. The process's measured effectiveness is 92 percent (92 ÷ 100).

Another way to evaluate how well an activity is organized is to measure how *efficiently* it uses resources; for example, measuring how efficiently an employee's time (resource) is used. This can be done by comparing the employee's actual performance against the ideal. Say for instance an employee is capable of performing 24 assorted activities in 240 minutes but that they actually only complete 20 activities during that time (the 20 activities at 10 minutes each represents 200 minutes of work completed). The employee's measured efficiency is calculated at 83 percent (200 minutes ÷ 240 minutes).

Or take how efficiently a piece of equipment is used (resource) to produce units. The equipment has the capacity to produce 100 units per hour. If it produces 80 units per hour, the equipment's measured efficiency is 80 percent (80 ÷ 100).

Management measures, analyzes, and evaluates how well each activity is organized using these two measures: effectiveness and efficiency. If an activity does not maximize results or resources, it gets reorganized.

Let me give you an example of evaluating organization using the Cell Subassembly Department (cited in the introduction to this book). Once the department's activities were identified and understood, I began to evaluate how well they maximized resources and results.

The cell subassembly process was organized around a conveyor system that delivered a plastic container to each cell assembler's workstation. A cell's unassembled parts filled the container representing a complete parts kit that, when assembled, would produce one of fifteen different cell configurations.

When the kit was received, the assembler identified the particular cell configuration so that he or she could retrieve the cell's individual assembly and wiring diagram. These diagrams were located in a filing cabinet next to the supervisor's desk (as much as forty feet away). The assembler would leave his or her workstation, walk to the filing cabinet, search for and hopefully find the right diagrams, and with these in hand, return to his or her workstation to begin assembling the cell.

When the cell was completed, it was placed on the conveyor belt taking it to the final assembly staging area. Then the whole process was repeated as another kit was delivered to the cell assembler's workstation. If the next cell kit matched the diagram in hand, the assembler remained at his or her workstation and began assembling the cell. If it did not match, the assembler had to once again walk to the filing cabinet to retrieve the appropriate diagrams.

I noticed that many assemblers left the filing cabinet empty-handed. There apparently were not enough cell diagram copies to go around. When this happened, assemblers returned to their workstations, returned the assigned cell kit, and asked the cell kit dispatcher for a different cell type, one whose diagrams were hopefully in the filing cabinet.

I asked one of the cell subassembly supervisors, "Why are there not enough assembly and wiring diagram copies to go around?"

"Engineering often changes the cell's specifications. When this happens, an entire set of assembly and wiring diagrams has to be photocopied. Management wants to limit how many copies we keep on hand to keep our copying costs down," the supervisor replied.

"Why are the copies kept at your desk and not nearer to the employees' workstations?" I asked.

"I need to have immediate access to the copies," the supervisor replied. "When engineering issues cell change orders, the old assembly and wiring diagrams must be replaced with the latest revision. Having them here near my desk gives me better control over doing this."

After evaluating how the cell assembly activities were organized, I concluded that resources were being wasted because of inefficient and ineffective organization. This conclusion prompted action. It was time to optimally organize the cell subassembly activities.

## Optimally Organizing Activities

As I began reorganizing the Cell Subassembly Department's activities, I did so without predeterminations or management-imposed limitations. I had two aims in mind: that resources were available so that activities could successfully be performed and that activities were organized so that resources were used effectively and efficiently.

For instance, I focused on the department's primary activity—assembling cells. In optimally organizing this activity, I made sure the resources an assembler required were readily accessible. This saved time, time that could be spent making more cells.

For example, the assembler's workstation was designed so an assembler would never have to leave it. Everything the assembler needed to assemble a cell was within easy reach—including all the wiring and assembling diagrams. To accomplish this, a binder was published for each assembler's workstation. The cost to provide these binders was negligible (several hundred dollars) compared to the much higher cost (in wasted assembler's time) of not having them at each workstation.

Thoroughly understanding the cell subassembly activities enabled me to evaluate how well they were organized and to arrive at an optimal solution that significantly contributed to the department's surge in productivity. Although arriving at optimal organizing solutions is sometimes obvious, this is not always the case. There are situations where arriving at optimal organization requires more penetrating analysis—analysis obtained through measuring how an activity maximizes resources and results.

Let me give you an example of how this approach leads to optimal organization. A large industrial sales company had hired my consulting firm to improve its performance and profitability. The company's sales were serviced through its central warehouse, where industrial supplies were received, stored, and shipped to the customer.

Envision a sprawling, cavernous warehouse. Throughout the facility's expanse was a forest of green steel racking, stretching thirty feet into the air. Situated on the racking were multiple rows of inventory items placed on wood pallets. Interspacing the racking were aisles and cross-aisles.

Traveling along these aisles were dozens of yellow forklifts whose operators picked up and put away inventory. The forklift operators began and ended their runs at the front loading docks where picked orders were loaded onto semitrucks and semitrucks were unloaded and newly received inventory put away.

To facilitate inventory item picking and putting away, the forklift operators received either an order picking ticket or an inventory placing ticket. These tickets specified the inventory items being moved, their respective quantity, and the item's warehouse bin location.

These tickets required the forklift operators to travel to various bin locations throughout the warehouse. The measured travel time to the far reaches of the warehouse took four minutes and another four minutes to return—an eight-minute round-trip. The shortest measured travel time was to inventory locations nearest the loading area that took only ten seconds to access—a twenty-second round-trip.

From all outward appearances, the warehouse seemed well organized. But was it optimally organized? To answer this question, I first recognized all of the department's activities. These were further broken down into their various parts, enabling me to thoroughly understand them.

Once I broke down the forklift operator's activities, I noted that the distance they had to travel to pick and put away items impacted whether they maximized resources and results. There was a direct correlation between the resources used (operator time, fuel and maintenance, etc.) and the results obtained (orders picked and items put away) and the distance traveled (ten seconds to four minutes). Was this organizing factor being considered?

I asked the warehouse manager, "How are the bin locations chosen for the inventory items?"

He replied, "The computer randomly assigns the inventory bin location based on a bin being available." Following up, I asked, "Is there a reason *why* the computer does not take into account how frequently items are picked and the distance a forklift driver has to travel?"

"Nope," he answered. "The computer software does not take that into account. It's done randomly based on an empty bin location being available, and it does not make any difference how far the bin is located from the loading area or how frequently an item is picked."

This answer told me that resources were probably not optimally organized. Randomly assigning inventory item locations meant the distance traveled had not been taken into account. If this were the case, then forklift operators were wasting valuable resources traveling farther distances than necessary.

To analyze whether this was the case, I measured how resources were being used. I did this by creating a report that listed all the items the company sold, how often these items were picked and replenished, and where each item was located in the warehouse.

As I scanned the report, there was nothing optimal about how the inventory locations were organized. They were indeed random. There was no organizing principle taking into account the frequency and distance a forklift operator had to travel and the respective resources this cost.

For example, an item that was frequently picked 12,434 times and replenished over 500 times (each pallet held twenty-four items) each year was located at the back of the warehouse. This required a forklift operator to make an eight-minute round-trip each time the item was picked or replenished. On the other hand, there was an inventory item that was picked only eighteen times a year. This item was located in a bin location next to the loading dock, requiring a forklift operator to make only a twenty-second round-trip.

The report also showed that the items the company sold predictably conformed to the Pareto principle. Approximately 20 percent of the warehoused items represented 80 percent of the company's sales volume. This was an important finding. It meant that frequently picked and restocked items required a proportionally smaller number of bin locations. These items therefore could be placed in bin locations nearest to the loading area to reduce the distance traveled. The less frequently picked and placed items, representing 80 percent of the total, could be located in bin locations farther away.

Based on these findings, we went about optimally reorganizing the warehouse to maximize resources. We chose to color-code each item based on its reported pick or place frequency. For example, an item that had a high pick or place frequency was coded red. An item that had a moderate pick or place frequency was coded green. An item that had a low pick or place frequency was coded blue. On a parallel track, we color-coded bin locations. Bin locations closest to the loading area were coded red, bin locations midway to the loading area were coded green, and bin locations farthest away from the loading area were coded blue.

Over the next several weeks, the red-coded items were moved in close to red-coded bin locations. Green- and blue-coded items were moved farther away to green- and blue-coded bin locations, freeing up choice (closer to the loading area) red bin locations. The green-coded items were placed in green-coded bins located midway throughout the warehouse. Blue-coded items were purposely placed in blue-coded bin locations farthest away from the loading area.

When the red-coded items were in place, it took a forklift operator between ten and sixty seconds to pick or replenish these frequently accessed items. Our organizing efforts had an immediate impact on the resources being used as forklift operators traveled far less. In just eight weeks, the warehouse staff's time utilization and productivity doubled and forklift fuel usage was cut in half.

## Organize Around the Most Valuable Resources

Finally, we will discuss one other organizing principle. In organizing optimally, it is crucial to favor the most valuable resources. An example of this was used to great effect in a faltering sales department. I was asked to consult a large business-to-business sales company to improve their sales effectiveness. I practiced organizing by recognizing, understanding and evaluating the activities salespeople performed. It soon became apparent that how the department was organized was fundamentally flawed, wasting one of the company's most valuable resources—their salespeople's capacity to make sales.

Because the most crucial resource to the company's success was the time the sales force spent selling products and services, it was essential that their time be organized to sell as much as possible. But unfortunately, a variety of administrative activities had been assigned to the salespeople. These non-selling activities not only took up their valuable time but also were activities that most sales professionals are not very good at. The company had other staff who could capably perform these functions, but because the department's activities had always been performed this way, the sales force's time was being squandered through ineffective organizing.

The department was optimally reorganized, focused on maximizing the salespeople's time. Non-sales-related activities were assigned to others. This gave the salespeople more time to sell, and sell they did. Sales in the next twelve months doubled, creating record sales and profits.

## Conclusion

Effective organizing results in maximizing the resources an activity employs and the results it produces. When activities are thus *optimally* organized, they help achieve an organization's aims.

But have all the activities been recognized, including the

activities' individual parts? Has management gained a thorough understanding of how the activities are performed? Have all the activities been optimally organized to maximize resources and results?

While the practice of organizing preemptively attempts to address these questions, it is not equipped to do so alone. Five more learned disciplines of management are required to fully answer these (and other essential) questions. Although one of these, measuring performance, has been introduced in this chapter, there is much more about this invaluable discipline to discover.

In the next chapter, we will explore more fully how measuring performance enables management to accurately determine how effectively and efficiently an activity is performed.

## Chapter 3

# Measuring Performance

What gets measured gets done.

—Tom Peters

Frederick W. Taylor published his seminal work *The Principles of Scientific Management* in 1911. The book was a groundbreaking effort to encapsulate management theory and practice, an approach Taylor called *scientific management*. The book was an immediate success, becoming the best-selling business book in the first half of the twentieth century, and is considered one of the most influential books on management ever published.[1]

Taylor is recognized as the first efficiency expert and management consultant. More importantly, he is the acknowledged founder of modern management. Taylor's management principles, presented in a book over a century ago, continue to influence how we manage today.

Taylor's career began in a Philadelphia machine shop in 1874 when he was eighteen years old. Hired as a lowly apprentice, he quickly rose through the management ranks in the bustling industrial age.

Early on, Taylor was determined to discover the principles of effective management. He approached this task doggedly and confidently. He had a way of seeing things, not as they were, but how they ought to be. He was a management innovator in discovering the means that would best realize the aims.

His approach to how things ought to be was methodical and systematic. He carefully observed work activities being performed, breaking them down into their various parts. He was able to thoroughly understand, measure, and analyze each activity and its collective parts, and once he identified the "one best way", Taylor constructed a management system to perpetuate its being performed in this way.

Taylor used performance measurement to not only determine the one best way but also to facilitate his management system. Consequently, measuring performance was integral to Taylor's "scientific" approach to managing—at the time, a controversial and misunderstood technique.

For example, in *The Principles of Scientific Management*, Taylor recounts his experience of introducing scientific management at Bethlehem Steel in 1899 where Bethlehem's management had asked Taylor to help them better manage the mill's workmen who manually moved materials used in making iron and steel.

Taylor began the consulting project observing workmen haplessly shoveling coal. As he did so, he noticed that sixteen different shovel sizes and shapes were being used and that this practice contributed to their poor performance. In fact, he noted that it was a common practice for workmen to haphazardly grab whatever shovel was at hand to move coal and other various materials without any thought about the size, shape, and weight of those materials. Taylor would go on to show that management's indifference to the kinds of shovels workmen used was inefficient and costly.

Taylor set about to find the best way to carry out this manual task. He began experimenting to determine what was the maximum weight a workman could shovel without getting overly tired. It was twenty-one pounds. Using this data, he investigated what kind of shovel could move twenty-one pounds of a given material. When this testing was complete, Taylor was able to match the right shovel with the appropriate material to maximize a workman's efficiency.

After determining the best way to shovel materials, Taylor timed how long the activity should take using twenty-one pounds per shovel load as the ideal measure. These performance standards would now be applied to each workman's actual work output, allowing management to gauge how the workmen performed.

The standards were applied using a shoveling management system Taylor had designed. The system worked like this: A workman reporting to the yard was issued (based on the kind of material he was assigned to move) one of ten shovel types. The amount of material the workman shoveled was recorded throughout the day and tallied. At workday's end, the actual total was compared to the ideal performance standard and the comparative results were given to each workman (using a color-coded card), giving him performance feedback. Workers who achieved the ideal performance standard were given pay bonuses. Workers whose performance was found wanting were encouraged to work harder. If, over time, a workman could not perform to the ideal, he was removed from shoveling duties.

Taylor's innovative approach to managing had immediate results as Bethlehem's shoveling labor costs were cut in half.

Throughout *The Principles of Scientific Management*, Taylor cites other successful examples where applying scientific management improved employee efficiency and organizational effectiveness. Integral to these accomplishments were Taylor's reliance on measuring performance.[2]

Although Taylor developed his management principles over one hundred years ago, their practice is relevant and applicable today. This is especially true of measuring performance, a central tenet to Taylor's pioneering efforts. Contemporary management author Tom Peters also emphasizes the importance of this often misunderstood discipline when he succinctly states, "What gets measured gets done."[3]

## Measuring Performance

Measuring performance is essential to management making the right things happen. Its practice allows management to evaluate how activities *should* be organized and performed. And its practice enables management to gauge how activities *are* organized and performed. This common feedback is essential. Allow me to illustrate.

Imagine going to the ballpark where you anticipate watching your favorite baseball team take on their archrivals in a close pennant race. As you are being seated, it is announced that tonight's game will be played using a new set of rules. The players' union, concerned for their members' well-being, has insisted on these rules as a way to reduce the stress caused by the game's unceasing pressure to perform. Baseball management has sympathetically agreed to the rules. As a result, tonight's game will be played without any performance measures.

Scanning the glossy program, you notice the batting averages for each player have been omitted. Gone too are the batters' other performance measures, such as the number of hits, singles, doubles, triples, home runs, strikeouts, and walks. You search in vain for the starting pitcher's earned run average and his win-loss record. Looking up at the scoreboard, you realize it has been turned off. The tracking of performance measures such as the number of balls, strikes, outs, and runs scored won't be done—it's deemed too stressful.

Taking the field, the players appear happy and relaxed. The new rules seem to be working. But then you notice the teams' managers. Apparently, the new rules have caused these managers a good deal of confusion and anguish. They appear utterly lost and befuddled, which is easy to understand. How do you manage without measuring performance?

A definitive score at the game's end is one of sports' most compelling aspects, for the score depicts how the team performed. Additionally, the many individual and team performance measures give managers feedback to manage effectively. Consequently, measuring performance gives the sports world clear, unmistakable, and unambiguous results whose interpretation is objective and conclusive.

This far-fetched trial baseball game sounds ludicrous, doesn't it? Not measuring performance would not only ruin one of America's favorite games, but it would also be the ruin of many a manager who tries to make the right things happen without keeping score. Effective management depends on keeping score. Keeping score entails measuring how an organization's key activities are performed. How activities are performed is not an academic question. For how well these activities are performed determines an organization's success (or failure), whether or not it's winning a game, teaching a child to read, or making a profit.

## What Is Measuring Performance?

Measuring performance functions much like the gauges on a car's dashboard. These gauges measure the car's performance and give the driver feedback to operate the vehicle. For example, the gauges measure how much gasoline is in the tank, the engine's operating temperature, and the car's speed.

Likewise, measuring performance gauges how key activities are performed. These measures give managers clear, immediate, and objective feedback, indicating how effectively and efficiently an activity was performed. With this performance information, management recognizes when an activity is performed poorly so that the appropriate action can be taken to address the situation.

Therefore, the discipline of measuring performance first encapsulates an activity's required performance dynamics. Next, these encapsulated performance dynamics are measured and translated into performance standards. Performance standards are comparative measures, much like the "FULL" notch on a car's gas gauge, that indicate the ideal. Finally, management measures how an activity is actually performed and contrasts this measure against the ideal. The result is binary (like a car's dashboard indicator lights where green is good and red indicates a problem). When actual measured performance is ideal, it indicates resources and results have been maximized.

When actual measured performance is not ideal, it indicates problems have occurred that have minimized results and wasted resources (e.g., a sale was lost, a customer dissatisfied, an employee's time wasted, or a defective product produced).

## Three Ways to Measure Performance

There are three ways to measure performance. They are time-based measures, outcome-based measures, and relational-based measures. Let's look at each of these in turn.

Time-based performance measures establish the time (usually in minutes) it ideally takes to complete a given activity. For example, a time-based performance measure indicates the number of minutes it takes an employee to process a customer's order or the number of minutes it takes an employee to assemble a product.

Outcome-based performance measures establish the number of outcomes an activity ideally produces. This is often stated within a time context. For example, an outcome-based performance measure indicates the number of units (outcomes) a machine produces in an hour or the number of sales calls (outcomes) a salesperson performs in a day.

Relational-based performance measures show how two or more performance measures ideally relate, depicted as a ratio, quotient, or some other relative, comparative amount. For example, the number of defective units produced in relation to the total number of units produced gives us a quality performance ratio. The number of minutes it actually took to complete an activity compared to the number of minutes it should have taken gives us an efficiency performance ratio.

An example of a more complex relational-based performance measure would be an algorithm that determines a department's staffing requirements. The algorithm would list all the activities the department performs, as well as the number of times each activity is performed during the year. The annual frequency of each activity would be multiplied by its time-based performance measure. These results are totaled and are divided by sixty minutes, resulting in the total number of employee hours the department's activities ideally require. This hour total is then divided by the department's actual performance efficiency. The result is the number of employee hours the department's activities demand. When this total is divided by the total annual number of hours an individual employee has available (less paid breaks, vacation, and sick time), it results in the number of employees required to staff the department.

## Measuring Performance Facilitates Management Practice

Measuring performance is an enabling discipline. It works integrally to facilitate practicing the other learned disciplines of management. Already we have seen how measuring performance works in conjunction with *planning* to establish measurable aims and means. We have seen how *organizing* uses measuring performance to evaluate whether an activity is organized optimally.

In the following chapters, we will see how *executing* uses performance measures to appropriately assign activities and engage and empower employees to perform activities ideally, how *following up* uses performance measures to ascertain how well an employee performed his or her assigned activities, how *real-time reporting* takes measured performance information and shares it throughout the organization, and how *problem solving* uses performance measurement to identify, understand, and solve problems.

As an example of how measuring performance facilitates the other management disciplines and empowers management effectiveness, consider the implications where an employee's measured performance over a two-hour period is only 50 percent. Although 60 of the 120 minutes were accounted for, what happened to the remaining 60 minutes? How was this missing 60 minutes used? Was the time wasted? Did problems consume the time? If so, what were the problems, and were they appropriately responded to? Was the time lost because of improper training? Did the employee have enough work to do? Did the employee have a bad day? Did the employee use this time doing personal, non-work-related activities?

When an employee's performance has been measured and found wanting, it raises questions that management must answer and address. Unless unacceptable performance is recognized and its source identified, management cannot take the appropriate action to address it. And not addressing unacceptable performance only perpetuates it as management allows the wrong things to happen.

## Why Measuring Performance Is Not Practiced

Given performance measurement's inestimable benefits, you would think its practice was universal. But sadly that is not the case. Let's take a moment to explore why performance measurement is not practiced.

Perhaps the chief reason measuring performance is not practiced is because its distinct qualities go unrecognized and unappreciated. As a result, other methods such as accounting information, simple activity tallies, and industrial time and motion studies are commonly substituted. These are inadequate substitutes at best.

Unlike these methods, measuring performance is designed to assess an activity's unique performance characteristics. This results in measured performance feedback that is clear, immediate, and objective. It takes distinct, quantifiable, and quantitative performance feedback to indicate how activities were performed. And it is this feedback that managers can instantly use to make the right things happen. Therefore, management cannot afford to use performance measurement substitutes that leave them uninformed as to how essential activities were performed; such substitutes are often inadequate methods that put managers in the dark as they try to piece together a performance puzzle without having the picture to do so.

Another reason why measuring performance is not practiced is its perceived difficulty. However, this is a misperception. It is not that measuring performance has been tried and found difficult but rather it has appeared difficult and never tried.

The perceived difficulty of measuring performance is often not in deriving performance measures themselves. In most cases, this is a simple and straightforward exercise (we will discuss how it's done later in this chapter). Rather, the perceived difficulty lies in overcoming the negative connotations that surround practicing measuring performance.

This assortment of detrimental perceptions is held by employees and managers alike. These parties seldom see performance measurement as a positive, beneficial practice. Instead, it is resisted and avoided, held in contempt and considered a threat. What is it about measuring performance that causes such reactions?

## Measuring Performance's Negative Perceptions

In organizations that do not practice this essential management discipline, it is easy to understand why measuring performance is resisted. Its practice profoundly changes the organization's performance dynamics. Measuring performance not only introduces ideal performance expectations but also measures the actual performance outcomes. How an individual performs becomes a known quantity—specifically, whether ideal performance has been obtained or not. If it has not, individuals are asked to account for their poor performance.

Measuring performance is relentless; it constantly, quantifiably, and qualitatively measures how activities are performed. It exposes individual performance, stripping away pretense, incompetence, and complacency. It is no surprise that measuring performance can be threatening, as poorly performing employees and managers have no place to run or hide.

Accountability issues aside, there are other disapproving reasons why performance measurement is not practiced. Some reasons are based on unpleasant past experiences where the discipline was misused or misunderstood. Other reasons are based in fact, as measuring performance brings on unpleasant realities. Additionally, there are other negative perceptions that are exaggerated, inaccurate, mistaken, and entirely false.

Let's take a closer look at some of these negative perceptions. It's important that these be understood so that they can be properly addressed and overcome. For the practice of measuring performance isn't optional, since an organization's success hinges on how effectively activities are managed and performed. How these activities are performed must not be left to chance, as managing without keeping score invites failure.

Negative perception #1: *Measuring performance treats people as cogs in a machine. It is a dehumanizing, callous practice that ignores work's human element. It reduces a person and the work he or she does to an abstraction—a thing.*

It is unfortunate that measuring performance is perceived as a dehumanizing management practice. For when this vital discipline is rightly practiced, employees do not feel like they are being treated as a cog in a machine, but instead that the work they do matters. This is an important consideration, for employees want their work contribution recognized and appreciated.

These are the results of a survey given to thousands of employees across the country asking them what makes their work most satisfying:

- Full appreciation of work being done
- Feeling of being in on things
- Help on personal problems
- Job security
- High wages
- Interesting work
- Promotion in the company
- Personal loyalty of supervisor
- Good working conditions
- Tactful discipline

The survey results reveal that "full appreciation of work being done" ranks as the most important quality, of all the qualities, in work satisfaction.[4] Measuring performance addresses this need as an individual's work performance is measured, recognized, and appreciated. Measuring performance fully and objectively recognizes each employee's work contribution. It reinforces the need that we all have for our work to be recognized and appreciated.

I recall an experience where measuring performance was introduced in a unionized distribution center. For the first time in the firm's twenty-five-year history, each employee's work performance was measured. After the first week, we posted the results for everyone to see. The posting predictably drew a crowd of curious employees. Listed on the report were each employee's name and respective weekly measured performance (stated as an efficiency percentage).

There was quite a disparity in the performance results. This no doubt led to the ribbing and joking that soon took place among the gathered employees. The highest score belonged to an employee we'll call Gavin. Gavin's performance was measured at a respectable 71 percent. This result was not a surprise—coworkers and management alike saw Gavin as the department's most capable and motivated employee. However, it was a disappointment to Gavin. He asked what was considered excellent. I told him anything above 90 percent. Afterward, he made certain his measured performance never fell below 90 percent as Gavin detested having his performance being considered only average.

The lowest score belonged to an employee we'll call Roger. Roger's measured performance was only 27 percent. This was not a surprise to Roger's coworkers. They knew of Roger's morning ritual where he drove his forklift, unbeknownst to management, to the remotest part of the warehouse. Once there, he would park, prop up his feet, sip his morning cup of coffee while reading the newspaper, and then invariably go to sleep. Roger's low measured performance reflected his morning ritual.

Overall, the response to the posting was positive and encouraging. The warehouse employees were no longer treated as cogs in a machine but as individuals whose work mattered. For the first time, their work performance was measured and recognized and this information was shared throughout the organization.

For those like Gavin whose work performance was exemplary, performance measurement led to being commended. Gavin's manager recognized his work performance and thanked him for a job well done. The company's owner also paid Gavin a visit thanking him for his excellent work.

Wayward Roger took note. He abandoned his morning ritual in an effort to achieve better performance. In a short time, his measured performance improved to a level comparable to his coworkers. Management's effort to measure and recognize performance gave employees like Roger newfound pride and satisfaction in their work when they realized that their work performance mattered.

Negative perception #2: *Management uses measuring performance as a heavy-handed method to extract more work from already overworked employees.*

Measuring performance, like any tool, can be misused. This happens when an employee's performance is manipulated to obtain unrealistic results. To avoid this misuse, management must establish performance measures that are a realistic, sensible, and practical. These are performance measures that can be achieved while an employee works in an ordinary, unhurried, and sustainable manner.

Negative perception #3: *Management measures performance because they mistrust their employees' motivation and intentions. This mistrust creates an adversarial and suspicious work environment that thwarts organizational effectiveness.*

Ronald Reagan is noted for his wise quip "Trust, but verify." This philosophy applies to measuring performance as well, for its practice incorporates these two seemingly contradictory but coexisting principles. Although most employees try their best, it is naive to assume that all do. It is also misguided to assume that an employee is in a job that best suits his or her abilities. Setting aside an employee's motivation and suitability, there are situations where the employee's inability to acceptably perform is related to circumstances outside the employee's control. In all these situations, measuring performance enables management to recognize and address the issues.

For example, I was turning around a troubled publishing company that was fast losing money. As part of the turnaround process, I scrutinized every expense in an attempt to increase profitability through reducing expenses. In doing so, I noticed that the company was spending several hundred dollars per week in overnight parcel post shipments. I asked why. I was told that the customer service representatives had incorrectly entered a customer's order. When this happened, the company was obligated to rush the correct, time-sensitive materials to the customer at the company's expense. At the time, I accepted this as a justifiable expense. However, I was soon to discover this was an incorrect assumption.

This discovery was made possible through practicing the learned disciplines of management, which were quickly deployed throughout the company. Now the company's managers had the tools they needed to manage more effectively, including measuring how each employee performed. This practice showed the primary reason for the parcel post shipping expenses.

Practicing measuring performance in the customer service department gave management feedback as to how each employee performed. Measured were how effectively and efficiently employees processed customer orders. This included each employee's order entry error rate. And it was this performance measure that brought to light a glaring discrepancy among the department's employees. One employee, whom we'll call Judith, was responsible for over 80 percent of the order entry errors.

Judith had been a long-serving (over ten years) customer service representative. Over that time, she had a reputation as a hard worker who processed the most orders. Because performance measurement had not been practiced, management did not know that Judith's prodigious productivity was misleading. However, once Judith's performance was actually known, her high order entry error rate and its costly consequences (costs included not only the overnight parcel post shipping expenses but also the wrongly shipped products that were written off, the additional warehouse and customer service employee time to process the correct customer order, and the displeased customers) overshadowed her seemingly commendable qualities.

Judith's manager immediately began remedial training and cautioned Judith to enter customer orders more carefully.

Unfortunately, these actions did not help improve Judith's performance. Subsequently, she was formally warned that unless her poor work performance improved, she would be transferred to another department.

Again, Judith's manager prevailed upon her to slow down and take more care in accurately entering orders and intensified her training, but to no avail, as she continued to enter orders incorrectly. The expenses incurred correcting Judith's errors continued unabated. After two months of measuring her performance, management concluded that Judith did not have the aptitude to satisfactorily perform her job. She was asked to take another position in a different department—an offer she refused. Consequently, she was fired because of her poor work performance.

A few weeks later, the Equal Employment Opportunity Commission (a governmental agency that enforces federal employment discrimination laws) notified management that Judith had filed an age discrimination complaint against the company. In the complaint, Judith accused management of firing her because of her age. In subsequent federal agency hearings, management had to defend their decision to fire Judith, proving that their action was not because of age discrimination. Fortunately, through the learned disciplines of management, they had measured and documented Judith's work performance. It was this data that supported the company's decision, clearly showing that Judith was fired because of her performance, not her age. The agency agreed, and the case was dismissed.

Negative perception #4: *It is not possible to accurately measure how well activities are performed. This skepticism stems from the belief that work activities are too complex and variable to be measured.*

Indeed, many work activities are complex and unpredictable and this sometimes makes measuring them challenging. However, it is not so challenging that it cannot be done. Although I have encountered complex and variable activities, I have always been able to effectively measure how they are performed.

That is not to suggest that all performance measures are the same. They can vary greatly. Nevertheless, deriving the right performance measure is possible (later in this chapter, I'll show you how).

Negative perception #5: *Measuring performance is a rigid and unrealistic management approach. It is based on how an activity could be done, not necessarily on how it should be done.*

Measuring performance is a rigid regimen. It determines the best way an activity should be performed and establishes an ideal performance measure based on the activity being performed in that manner. Admittedly, performing the activity ideally is not always possible, especially when problems arise. But the presence of problems should not deter management from striving to have the activities performed ideally.

For example, performance measurement was introduced into an accounting department. One activity—processing the company's accounts receivable transactions—could best be completed using a four-step process that took thirty seconds. Using this process represented the ideal, maximizing resources and results.

An employee we'll call Irene was assigned the activity of processing accounts receivable transactions using this four-step process. When management followed up on Irene's performance, it was half of what it should have been. I was asked to confirm whether the established ideal performance measure was correct.

Investigating Irene's low performance, I was able to confirm the performance measure was indeed correct. It turned out the reason for Irene's poor performance was her insistence on performing the activity how she'd always done it—using six steps, not four. Irene contended that her way was better despite the fact it took twice as long. Irene was not performing the activity using the best method. It took her manager's intervention to get her to use the four-step process. When she finally did, her measured performance doubled as expected.

Negative perception #6: *Measuring performance against an ideal creates an unrealistic expectation. Perfect performance is not possible in the real world.*

Measuring performance does create an artificial and unrealistic expectation. It expects activities to be performed perfectly, an expectation that admittedly runs counter to how the real world operates. In the real world, problems arise and circumstances conspire to make achieving ideal performance difficult if not impossible. So when actual performance is measured and compared to ideal performance, it highlights a disparity. This disparity or performance gap indicates that problems have occurred, and it is these problems that serve as a goad for management to make the right things happen and, over time, results in the ideal becoming more realistic.

This is an important principle to stress. Measuring performance compares and contrasts actual performance against ideal performance measures. This signifies whether ideal performance was obtained. If not, it highlights something went wrong. The wrong things are problems that must be addressed so that ideal performance can be achieved.

I recall developing performance measures for a technical service department. When I presented the results to the department's manager and technicians, I was told that the performance measures were not realistic, that they were impossible to achieve. I agreed, but I pointed out that problems made them unrealistic. I added that once the problems could be identified, understood, and addressed, the department's performance would improve, making the performance measures possible. Begrudgingly, the department's manager assented to having the department's performance measured using these "unrealistic" performance standards.

After the first week, it appeared they were right. The

department's measured performance was only 22 percent compared against ideal. But measuring performance in this way highlighted a 78 percent performance gap. The reasons for the gap disclosed a laundry list of problems. Once these problems were addressed, the department's performance improved. In a few months' time, the "impossible measures" were regularly being achieved and fast becoming the norm as the department's measured performance climbed to over 80 percent.

This improvement would never have happened without ideal performance measures. It took these "unrealistic" measures to identify the performance gap that existed between ideal and actual performance. The performance gap spurred management action, causing problems to be appropriately addressed, which narrowed the gap.

Negative perception #7: *Measuring performance places high expectations on employees and managers alike. When they are unable to meet these performance expectations, undue stress and unwanted conflict result.*

Expecting personnel to perform at a high level and holding them accountable when they don't is stressful and conflict-ridden. Unfortunately, stress and conflict are necessary by-products when addressing problems that negatively impact performance. Fortunately, these by-products are often constructive (and lessen over time), since they cause performance to improve. This result is opposite to those organizations that do not practice performance measurement. In these organizations, stress and conflict also arise (and rarely subside) and seldom are constructive as the organization wallows in mediocrity and failure.

Negative perception #8: *Measuring performance is not kind or understanding. It does not take into account life difficulties and how these impact an individual's performance.*

This is true. Measuring performance reduces performance to a number. It does not take into account the personal difficulties we all go through such as illness, loss of a pet, or being up all night nursing a sick child. Therefore, it is incumbent on management to use performance measures wisely; which includes concern for both an employee's performance results and their well-being.

Negative perception #9: *Measuring performance requires extra time and effort. It adds to employees' and managers' already overloaded work demands and cannot be done without causing other more important work to suffer.*

Practicing performance measurement does require additional time and effort, but so does not practicing performance measurement. The difference is when performance measurement is not practiced, additional time and effort is taken up reacting to unending problems instead of constructively solving them. When measuring performance and the other learned disciplines of management are practiced, they empower management to solve problems, which frees up more time and effort to practically practice them.

Negative perception #10: *Measuring performance emphasizes productivity at the expense of quality. It stresses how much, not how well.*

Rightly done, measuring performance stresses both how much and how well. It does not stress one performance aspect over the other but gauges how efficiently (how much) and effectively (how well) an activity is performed. These aspects are not mutually exclusive; both can and should be performed simultaneously.

## How to Measure Performance

Having discussed the impediments to measuring performance, let's turn our attention to how it is practiced.

The first step is to establish an ideal performance measure for every activity. Deriving an ideal performance measure is a simple process. It entails measuring an activity that is performed ideally (that is using the best practices while not encountering any problems). This activity is measured (using time, outcome, and relational measures) to derive an ideal performance measure. Ideal performance measures are the essential building blocks that management uses to gauge how effectively and efficiently an activity is performed.

For example, deriving performance measures for the Cell Subassembly Department (related in chapter 1) required observing and measuring fifteen different cell types being assembled. I chose to use a time-based measure because it was the assembler's time that contributed to the activity's successful performance.

I carefully observed (making sure the best practices were employed) an assembler assembling each cell type while measuring how many minutes it took to complete. My aim was to collect enough timed-based observations to form a representative sample. This sample would then be used to derive the ideal performance measure for each cell type. The measure represented how many minutes it took an assembler to complete a particular cell type using the best methods and without incurring any problems.

If, when observing a cell being assembled, I noticed the assembler had encountered a problem, I made sure this time was excluded. I also was careful to note if the employee being timed was working at a normal pace. If I noticed the employee rushing or going unduly slow, I would adjust my timed observation accordingly or start over.

Deriving ideal activity performance measures for cell assembly required numerous timed observations. I intentionally observed various assemblers who had differing degrees of experience and skill. This diversity would allow me to derive performance measures that represented the entire department's capability (as opposed to focusing on a select few assemblers whose skill and experience was not a representative cross sampling).

I was eager to observe any problems the assemblers encountered or any best practices they used. These were documented so that the problems could be addressed and the best practices incorporated later on.

When I was confident I had collected enough timed observations to form a representative sample, I moved on to the next cell type. This confidence emerged when my observed times coalesced, indicating I had captured the activity's performance characteristics.

If my observed times did not coalesce—that is, the timed observations varied significantly—I made more timed observations to discover what accounted for the variation. Often this probe highlighted a problem or a best practice. At other times, it reflected the skill or experience disparity among the assemblers. If this was the case, I would collect more timed observations knowing that I would have to rely on a timed observation average for the ideal performance measure.

When I finished measuring the assembly of the fifteen different cells, I had collected on the low end approximately fifty timed observations for infrequently produced cell types and on the high end over two hundred timed observations for frequently produced cell types.

As a general rule, the more timed observations the better. Not only does gathering more timed observations make the sample more accurate, but it also provides valuable insight into how the activity is and should be performed. But at some point, making timed observations reaches a point of diminishing returns. This happens when no new times are collected—when no additional problems are observed and when no other best practices are discovered. This point usually arrives after a practical understanding of the activity being performed has been obtained. This understanding marks the time to move on and observe and measure the next activity.

While taking performance measurements is no secret, I have found discretion the best approach. So I try to be as inconspicuous as possible when measuring activities, for example, using the department's wall clock or glancing at my wristwatch to note how long an activity took. Not drawing attention to measuring performance minimizes making employees nervous, which helps gather accurate times.

Sometimes taking accurate performance measurements is not possible. For instance, this is especially challenging when employees know their performance is being measured and are uncomfortable with or opposed to the practice. Or the employee being observed cannot ideally perform the activity (because he or she is improperly trained or lacks the skills to do so). Under these circumstances, it is not possible to observe the activity being performed ideally.

In these cases, it's necessary to ask for the department's manager's help. This may require having the manager him or herself or a more willing and capable employee perform the activity so that accurate performance measures can be obtained.

Fortunately, I was able to make my cell subassembly observations discretely. After several weeks, I had collected sufficient observations to derive ideal performance measures for each activity.

For each cell, I derived an ideal performance measure using the timed observations I had collected. For example, cell type 201-A had timed observations measured in minutes (this is a partial list): 2.3, 2.2, 2.4, 2.5, 2.3, 2.6, 2.1, 2.4, 2.3, and 2.2. From these timed observations, an average was struck, resulting in a 2.3-minute ideal performance measure to assemble cell type 201-A.

An assembler's performance efficiency could be ascertained using this ideal measure. For instance, if an assembler completed 100 of type 201-A cells, he earned 230 minutes (100 cells x the 2.3-minute performance measure). The assembler's earned minutes were then divided by total minutes worked (excluding breaks), which in this case totaled 420 minutes. This resulted in the assembler's performance being measured at 55 percent (230 minutes ÷ 420 minutes).

An assembler's effectiveness (quality scorecard) was also measured. For instance, tracked were the number of defective cells assembled compared to the total number of cells assembled. If an assembler assembled 100 of type 201-A cells and, out of these, 5 were defective, the assembler's effectiveness was measured at 95 percent (100 total cells assembled ÷ 95 defect-free cells).

Here is another example of deriving performance measures that took place in a customer service department. I had recognized (through organizing) twenty-six different activities the department performed.

For each of these activities, I took numerous timed observations. For example, one activity I observed and measured was called "Process Customer Credit." After collecting fifty timed observations, here is part of my data: 35 seconds, 40 seconds, 37 seconds, 35 seconds, 32 seconds, 43 seconds, 38 seconds, 35 seconds, 30 seconds, 32 seconds, 35 seconds, 40 seconds, 37 seconds, 35 seconds, 32 seconds, 43 seconds, 38 seconds, 35 seconds, 30 seconds, 32 seconds. The variation in the timed observations was so small (consisting of 12 seconds) that I chose not to conduct more observations. Averaging my timed observations resulted in a 35.7-second standard. I rounded to the nearest tenth of a minute, setting 0.7 minutes as the activity's derived ideal performance measure.

Although there was a 12-second variation in the "Process Customer Credit" activity, this time variation was insignificant because of the activity's low frequency. The activity was performed, on average, two times per day. If the activity incurred a 12-second variation each time it was performed, it would add up to 24 seconds. This is not an amount of time worth considering. However, not all variations are insignificant.

Where an activity's time variation or frequency is significant, it makes understanding the variation worthwhile.

For example, in the same department I took timed observations of the activity "Incoming Customer Inquiries." My collected data after ten observations was 1 minute and 30 seconds, 30 seconds, 5 minutes and 11 seconds, 2 minutes, 2 minutes and 15 seconds, 4 minutes and 7 seconds, 3 minutes and 40 seconds, 35 seconds, 46 seconds, 2 minutes and 25 seconds.

The variation between my timed observations was significant, representing almost 5 minutes. I needed to delve deeper into understanding the activity more fully. To do so, I collected one hundred additional timed observations. These additional observations resulted in my better understanding the activity. The activity "Incoming Customer Inquiries" was too broadly defined to be accurately measured. Consequently, the activity was broken down into two separate activities. The first activity was for "General Incoming Customer Inquiries." These general inquiries were given a 1-minute performance measure. The second activity, "Specific Customer Inquiries," was given a 5-minute performance measure.

It should be noted that whenever an ideal performance measure is based on an average of timed observations, it has the potential to produce short-term variations in measured performance results. However, this inaccuracy over time (e.g., eight hours or forty hours) will diminish as the average accrues, making the measured performance results accurate.

Having discussed time-based performance measures, let's finally take up outcome-based performance measures. In deriving outcome-based measures, it is important to consider which outcome to measure. Take, for example, software developers writing code. Management could identify several different activity outcomes to measure. For instance, management could identify and measure the number of keystrokes performed. But this would be the wrong outcome to measure, for it does not fully capture the activity's performance characteristics. A better outcome selection would be the number of lines of code written. Measuring this outcome would pragmatically capture this activity's work content.

Once the proper activity outcome is selected, management observes and measures the activity being performed to derive the ideal number of outcomes. Let me give you an example of how selecting and measuring outcomes is done.

I was hired to turn around a large struggling sales department. I knew that effectively managing the department's salespeople required suitable sales performance measures. To accomplish this required that I do two things: first, determine how a salesperson's performance should be measured and, second, derive ideal performance measures to ideally measure the performance.

In analyzing the salespeople's activities, it became apparent that outcome-based performance measures best captured their main activity's performance characteristics—that of performing sales calls. It was this activity that produced sales, the department's chief aim.

Having settled on an outcome-based performance measure, I set about to derive an ideal performance measure for this activity. I carefully observed the sales process, including how long it took a salesperson to prepare for a sales call, the amount of travel time required to get to and from the customer's location, the time it took to perform the sales call, the time involved to prepare sales quotes, the time it took to process a customer's order, and the time required to follow up with the customer. When I took all these sales processes into account, I was able to determine that performing five sales calls per day was the ideal sales performance measure.

To effectively manage how the salespeople performed these five daily sales calls, more outcome-based performance measures were added to sales management's dashboard. These included the number of sales calls a salesperson actually completed, the number of customer price quote requests the sales calls generated, the number of sales orders the price quotes produced, the total number of sales orders generated, and the total number of sales dollars generated. Sales management used these performance measures to manage the salespeople's performance, increasing sales 100 percent in the coming year.

## Correcting Wrong Performance Measures

Keep in mind that despite your best efforts to derive accurate performance measures, you may end up arriving at the wrong one. This will mean having to go back and redo it. For example, in the customer service department discussed previously where twenty-six performance measures were derived, it turned out that not all were correct. I had derived a three-minute performance measure for an activity. But the department's manager told me it was too low. I agreed to recheck it. I went back to the department and observed and timed the activity again. Only this time I realized I had missed an important step that took another two minutes. The manager was right: the measure was too low. It was immediately changed to five minutes.

There are also times when an employee believes the performance measure is not accurate when in fact it is. Sometimes averages have to be explained, and sometimes the employees have to see for themselves how long an activity takes. Wendy, a customer service representative, complained that a forty-second time measure to process a customer credit was not realistic. Wendy and I met, and with a stopwatch in hand I asked her to perform the activity while I timed it. When she was done and looked up, I stopped the watch—it read thirty-seven seconds. "Wow!" Wendy exclaimed. "I was certain it took longer than that." Taking Wendy through the process allowed her to see for herself the validity of the forty-second time measure.

Performance measures are further tested, corrected, and

validated when the other learned disciplines of management are practiced. For example, I had derived performance measures for a medium-sized distribution center. The customers' orders were shipped using a company truck or parcel post. To process a parcel post order, I had established a five-minute performance measure.

But afterward, I saw the distribution center's *real-time reporting*. The employee who processed the parcel post shipments had a whopping 135 percent measured productivity performance. It was at that moment when I realized I had derived the wrong performance measure. It's not possible to perform above 100 percent. I returned to the department and took more timed observations of the activity. When I did, I recognized I had significantly overstated how long one of the activity's processes actually took. A new, more accurate time measure soon replaced the wrong one.

I cite these examples not to emphasize my fallibility but to point out that deriving performance measures is a process. The process obviously entails trying to get them right the first time. But another part of the process is to actually use the measures and, in doing so, validate them (or not). For credibility's sake, it is important to try and make them as accurate as possible. But when this does not happen, realize they are easy to correct later on in the process.

### Install a Performance Measurement Administrator

Once performance measures are in place, it is a good idea to make someone responsible for administering them. Existing measurements need to be maintained, validated, and if necessary, corrected. Also, activities change, requiring new measures to be derived. Administering performance measures is an ongoing effort.

For example, the need for an administrator arose when I was auditing a client's management team. The learned disciplines of management had been deployed for six months. Now I was asked to assess how the management team was adhering to their practice. While the audit was underway, I noticed a curious development in the Technical Service Department.

For many months, the measured performance of the department's technicians had plateaued at 50 percent. Then, inexplicably, their measured efficiency immediately shot up to over 70 percent. Investigating this development, I asked the department's manager how he had improved performance so dramatically and in such a short time.

His explanation was simple and unapologetic. He had changed the performance measures. He and his technicians had grown weary trying to make improvements in how the department performed against the ideal measures. This was especially grating as the other departments had made steady progress at improving their performance, whereas the Technical Service Department's performance improvement had stalled out. The department's problems were challenging to identify and difficult to solve.

In response to the growing pressure to improve his department's performance, the manager capriciously changed how performance was measured. He arbitrarily increased performance measures and inflated the number of activities performed to show a bogus performance improvement.

As a result of the audit, the manager's machinations and pretensions were dismantled. The previous performance measures were reintroduced. This caused the department's measured performance to plummet, forcing management to try once again to identify and address the problems. Eventually, the department did improve, but it took longer because of the intractable nature of the problems the department confronted.

## Conclusion

How an organization performs essential activities is crucial to its success. This performance cannot be left to chance, but is measured—recognizing what gets measured, gets managed, and gets done—as management acts on the performance feedback it receives to achieve ideal performance.

However, before the activities are carried out and their performance measured, it is crucial that the employees who are responsible for performing the activities are engaged and empowered to perform them ideally. This modus operandi of engaging and empowering employees is central to practicing the next learned discipline of management we turn to—executing.

## Chapter 4

# Executing

A leader's role is to raise people's aspirations for what they can become and to release their energies so they will try to get there.

—David Gergen

Executing is management personified. Executing involves managers taking concrete action to make an organization's abstract aims a reality. Execution's concrete actions includes; making sure all the essential activities are satisfactorily performed and completed, engaging employees to ideally perform their assigned activities, and empowering employees to overcome the problems they encounter. The tangible results of effective executing is management making the right things happen.

Executing is not only an imperative management discipline, it is also a pivotal one. Planning, organizing, and measuring performance lay the foundation for its practice. Executing in turn facilitates the practice of following up, real-time reporting, and problem solving.

Executing is simple in concept and demanding in practice. Conceptually, it entails carrying out all the activities that achieve the organization's aims. Its practice demands that the performance of these activities is not haphazard but is methodically assigned to those responsible for performing them.

Consequently, executing is a meticulous nuts-and-bolts discipline. It achieves the organization's aims by linking the desired outcomes to the activities that produce them. This makes executing certain, expectant, and compelling. Executing is certain because it identifies and assigns specific activities to be completed. Executing is expectant because it expects all the activities to be performed perfectly. Executing is compelling because it holds accountable those who are responsible for performing the activities, insisting on excellent performance.

This is a lot to ask from a management discipline and it is why practicing executing is so crucial.

## Executing Ineffectively Practiced

Unfortunately, many organizations do not skillfully practice executing. For some, its practice is not possible because the facilitating disciplines of planning, organizing, and measuring performance are not practiced.

For other organizations, executing is not done because other inadequate means are used in its place. For example, management commonly uses communication as a means to execute its aims. In these organizations, managers believe that if they emphasize the organization's vision, mission, and values, these oft-repeated qualities will work their way into how activities are performed. As if through a form of osmosis, communicating will effectively impact how activities are carried out and thus enable an organization to achieve its aims.

Not that communicating vision, mission, and values isn't important—it is. But it is a poor substitute for executing. For simply communicating an organization's aims will not tangibly bring them into existence.

Still, other organizations depend on an incomplete set of management disciplines, hoping these will enable managers to carry out the organization's aims. For instance, some organizations rely on planning. In these organizations, management believes that the right plan will allow them to accomplish the organization's aims. But planning is not executing. Its practice cannot achieve certain, expectant, and compelling performance outcomes.

An example of management's futile reliance on planning

to execute was illustrated for me at a struggling southwestern manufacturing company. The company designed and constructed commercial furniture. But despite its innovative designs, growing sales, and well-crafted plans, the company failed to effectively execute. Recognizing the need for more effectual management, the company's CEO engaged my firm.

During the consulting project's first weeks, we analyzed the company's performance. We discovered that expenses, especially labor and material costs, were spiraling out of control. Further, we realized the company was not productive. The plant's employees struggled to timely construct the furniture. This was reflected in the company's failure to meet customers' promised delivery dates. These dates were fictions as the plant typically shipped a customer's order three or more weeks past its due date.

The company's failure to produce the furniture it sold was not static. Each day the plant slipped further behind in its planned production schedule, causing order backlog to swell. It was now taking the plant nine weeks to fulfill an order, while the industry standard was three weeks. The management team's inability to execute its planned aims was proving costly, contributing to the company's mounting losses (which were approximately 10 percent of sales).

Amid all the negative findings, we did discover one positive: management produced excellent plans. But, unfortunately, these plans were used to execute, and it was this practice that caused many of the plant's problems.

Using a plan to execute activities meant giving department managers a weekly production plan. These plans spelled out for each department what activity outcomes were expected. For example, the plan indicated how many seat cushions to produce or how many furniture models to assemble. That was it. Planning was the only management discipline this management team practiced. The absence of the other six learned disciplines of management and, in particular, executing was telling.

Not practicing organizing resulted in activities being poorly organized. I watched a machine operator make parts for furniture that had not been ordered. When he was done, he had made a two-month supply. Meanwhile, parts had yet to be made for furniture that had already been sold and was already several weeks late on its promised delivery date.

Employee performance was not measured, so management had no objective way to gauge how well activities were performed. I observed an inadequately trained employee trying to perform her assigned tasks. It took her twice as long to accomplish the task as it should have taken. When the parts were completed, they were passed on to final assembly. However, the assemblers rejected 20 percent of the parts she had made because they were defective. This poor performance went unmeasured, unnoticed, and unmanaged.

There was no executing. Instead, each manager was expected to take his or her weekly plan and accomplish the stated aims. As a result, the weekly plan did not specify what activities needed to be performed, nor did it link their being satisfactorily carried out. Consequently, many essential activities were overlooked, not assigned, and never performed. Of those activities that were assigned, unfortunately they were performed without employees being engaged and empowered to excellently perform the activities. The result: demoralized and apathetic employees who accepted problems as just another frustrating part of their jobs as they muddled on.

There was no following up except when problems arose and management had to intervene. This happened frequently, as problems were rampant, requiring managers to react to the latest crisis amid the unending chaos.

Without following up, no real-time reporting was generated, precluding the sharing of actionable feedback. Instead, each week the various department managers crossed off their completed work assignments, returning this "report" to the plan's issuer.

Management's failure to practice these essential disciplines led to their greatest shortcoming—their inability to solve problems. This shortcoming perpetuated poor performance, contributing to the company's inability to successfully achieve its aims.

Given these management shortcomings, our consulting team quickly developed and deployed the seven learned disciplines of management. Practicing these disciplines transformed how the company was managed and performed.

Now management was able to effectively execute activities, which led to successfully fulfilling the organization's aims. Employees were engaged and empowered, resulting in problems being identified and addressed. When this happened, employees' measured productivity doubled. This twofold productivity increase allowed more activities to be completed (while using fewer resources), which led to more orders being shipped. In two months time, customer order backlog went from nine weeks' lead time to just three days. The company was soon making a 10 percent profit on sales (instead of losing 10 percent).

As this case underscores, there is no substitute for effective executing.

## Four Aspects of Executing

There are four aspects that make effective executing possible. These aspects help ensure that the organization's essential activities are satisfactorily performed. They are developing a checklist to identify and help carry out essential activities, properly assigning activities to the employees responsible for performing them, engaging employees to perform the assigned activities ideally, and empowering employees to deal with the problems that hinder their performance. Let's look more closely at each of these four aspects.

## *Developing a Checklist*

Performing essential activities cannot be left to chance. Therefore, it is incumbent on management to guarantee that all essential activities will be satisfactorily performed and completed. To ensure that this is done, management develops a checklist.

Checklists are basic tools used to identify and help carry out activities. They run the gamut from simple checklists used for cooking (recipes) to complex checklists used to operate nuclear power plants (nuclear reactor checklists).

The aviation industry in particular has embraced checklists—elevating them to iconic status. Pilots use checklists to identify and help them perform key activities to achieve a safe, effective, and efficient flight.

However, pilots have not always recognized the need for checklists. In fact, before the mid-1930s, they were not commonly used. The story of how pilots came to depend on checklists gives us insight into their practical value. Tragically, an accident over seventy-five years ago inaugurated their use.

In 1934, the US Army Air Corps realized that its current operational bomber, the B-10, was inadequate to wage modern warfare. The B-10's mission capability was limited. It only had a 1,200-mile range while carrying a 2,000-pound bomb payload.

The Army Air Corps command instead wanted a more capable bomber, one that could fly much longer distances at higher speeds while carrying an equal or greater bomb payload. So in the summer of 1934, the Army Air Corps proposed the development of a new frontline bomber to replace the outdated B-10.

The army had in mind a long-range bomber capable of flying 2,200 miles nonstop at a speed of at least 200 miles per hour while carrying a 2,000-pound bomb payload. The prototype had to be ready for a flight competition in October 1935.

Three aircraft manufacturers entered the competition: Boeing, Douglas, and Martin. Each quickly began developing a new bomber. Although the B-10 bomber was a practical two-engine design, Boeing engineers discreetly inquired whether the army would consider a more complex and capable four-engine bomber. Yes, they were told, if all the army's performance criteria was met.

Working in total secrecy, Boeing engineers sought to develop a bomber prototype that was not marginally better than the B-10 but radically better. They designated their new, groundbreaking design Model 299.

A year later, Model 299 was ready for its maiden test flight. The new aircraft was unlike any other bomber. Its speed, size, weight, armament, sleek design, long range, large payload, sophisticated technology, and four engines created a sensation. When a Seattle newspaper reporter caught sight of Model 299, he promptly called it a "flying fortress." The name stuck, capturing the plane's formidable appearance.

After more testing, Model 299 flew from Seattle to Dayton for the army competition. Upon landing, the Boeing flight crew was surprised to find no Army Air Corps officials were there to greet them. It turned out that no one was expecting them to arrive for at least another hour. Model 299 had averaged an unheard-of 232 miles per hour on its 2,100-mile nonstop flight—setting a world record.

Although Martin and Douglas had developed capable two-engine designs, Boeing's Model 299 Flying Fortress was in a class by itself. It could fly higher, faster, and nearly twice as far. Its four engines generated 4,800 horsepower, giving the bomber a maximum speed of 302 miles per hour. It had an 1,850-mile range (2,590 miles using auxiliary fuel tanks) while carrying a 10,000-pound bomb payload. In all respects, its performance dwarfed the competition's entries. It appeared Boeing had already been declared the winner before the flight competition even began.

On October 30, 1935, Model 299 was readied for the army's test flight. At the bomber's controls was the Army Air Corps chief test pilot Major Ployer P. Hill. A crowd of army officials, manufacturing executives, and reporters gathered to watch Boeing's bomber compete for the coveted army contract.

The sleek bomber roared down the runway and lifted off. It then began to climb steeply—too steeply—and then it stalled, rolled on its side, and fell out of the sky. On ground impact, it burst into flames. The crash killed Major Hill and another crew member.

Investigators sought to determine what had caused the fatal crash. They discovered it was not because of structural failure, engine breakdown, or a systems malfunction. Instead, they concluded the crash was caused by pilot error. Prior to takeoff, Major Hill had forgotten to release a spring lock to free the elevator and rudder controls. The locked controls made the aircraft impossible to fly. Thus Hill could not control the bomber's steep climb before its wings stalled and the plane crashed.

In the crash's aftermath, some believed that Boeing had developed an aircraft impossible to fly. A pilot had to attend to a myriad of activities, including monitoring four engines, each having its own fuel-air mix; regulating the pitch of the propellers; operating the retractable landing gear and wing flaps; and managing the control surfaces through stick, rudder, and trim tab inputs and other tasks (including releasing the control lock prior to takeoff). Some newspaper reporters dubbed the complex Boeing bomber as "too much plane for one man to fly."

The disaster had far-reaching consequences. Douglas was declared the competition's winner, receiving a contract for 133 aircraft. Boeing's Model 299 was deemed dangerously impractical.

Having depleted the company's cash in developing the new bomber, Boeing executives were desperate for a major army contract to stay in business. Now the Flying Fortress and the company that had developed it faced an uncertain future. However, a small group of die-hard Army Air Corps officers provided a glimmer of hope. They saw Model 299's potent potential and wanted to give Boeing another chance to keep its bomber program alive. Therefore, they ordered thirteen aircraft for further testing.

However, it was understood that a solution to safely pilot the bomber had to be found. The army officers made it clear that should any test aircraft suffer another crash, Boeing's bomber program would be doomed. Thereafter test pilots and Boeing engineers got together to try to solve the problem of safely piloting the Model 299 prototypes.

The most obvious solutions would have been to either simplify the aircraft or increase the training a pilot would undergo. However, neither of these solutions was practical. As for making the aircraft less complex, it was Model 299's complexity that contributed to its exceptional performance. Furthermore, the individual activities a pilot had to perform were not difficult. Rather, the challenge was in properly executing them.

As for more pilot training, it was inconceivable to try to train pilots to Major Hill's level and qualifications. In addition to being a college-trained engineer, Major Hill had eighteen years of flying experience. This included test piloting nearly sixty different aircraft for the Army Air Corps. When Major Hill took the controls of Model 299, he was the army's chief of flight testing.

In light of these limitations, the test pilots and engineers turned to a simple solution to safely pilot the Boeing bomber—a checklist. In fact, they created four checklists: for takeoffs, landings, taxiing, and flight. The checklists were simple and concise, listing in order the activities a pilot had to perform. For example, in preparing Model 299 for takeoff, the pilot must confirm the instruments are set, make sure the door and windows are closed, unlock the elevator control, release the brakes, and so on.

Using these checklists, test pilots logged 9,200 flying hours (flying approximately 1.8 million miles) in the test aircraft without one incident. This track record finally convinced the army brass that Model 299 was not too much airplane for one man to fly. In 1938, the army placed more orders for Boeing bombers, numbering the aircraft B-17. Eventually, they ordered 12,731 Flying Fortresses. The B-17 gave the Army Air Corps a potent, modern bomber. When World War II broke out, the B-17 enabled the United States to mount a successful bombing campaign against Nazi Germany, destroying its war-making capacity.[1]

Begun in 1935 and used ever since, checklists have given pilots a tool to help them execute activities, contributing to the aviation industry's stellar safety performance record. However, it is not only pilots who must carry out numerous complex and varied activities. Many work activities today have these same characteristics, making checklists an indispensible tool in their execution.

Therefore, it is incumbent on management to develop checklists. The checklist's purpose is to make certain that all essential activities will be carried out, to insure that their execution is not random. Consequently, a checklist is used to choreograph performance. It links identified activities into being assigned and performed. For those performing the activities, a checklist informs, directs, reminds, and records their efforts. For those managing the activities, a checklist records how the assigned activities have been performed, facilitating following up, real-time reporting, and problem solving.

Developing a checklist first requires recognizing all the activities an organization must perform to achieve its aims (a process carried out through the practice of organizing, as discussed in chapter 2). Next, it is decided which of these activities are to be assigned to individual employees to carry out. A checklist is then composed based on this final compilation of individually assigned activities and issued to the respective employee.

Checklists can be published in various forms (e.g., printed on paper or entered on an electronic spreadsheet). A copy of a paper-printed checklist developed for a customer service department (titled a "Daily Performance Report") is shown on page 104.

This checklist consists of a header and five columns. In the header is a space for the employee's name and the date. In the left column ("Category") are all the identified activities that have been assigned to be performed. In this case, there are thirty-four identified activities necessary to achieve the department's aims.

The next column ("Total") is used to record the activities that have been completed. The "Problems" column is used to document any problems that were encountered. The "C" column allows for the kind of problem to be quickly coded. The final column ("TLT") is used to record the total lost time each problem caused.

Each customer service representative was issued this checklist and asked to use it to carry out their assigned activities. The checklist orchestrated performance, controlling how essential activities were assigned and performed. As the checklist was updated throughout the day, the employee and his or her manager had a record of which activities had been completed (and which were not). This simple checklist took the guesswork out of performance outcomes, enabling this particular customer service department to achieve its organizational aims.

## *Assigning Activities*

The developed checklist is now used to facilitate the second aspect of executing: formally assigning specific activities to particular employees to perform. This is a crucial step, for when managers are unable or unwilling to make formal, specific work assignments to individual employees, the activity's performance outcome is uncertain and unpredictable. This is not effective executing but wishful thinking.

Instead, effective executing requires management to formally

## INSIDE SALES REPRESENTATIVE
## DAILY PERFORMANCE REPORT

Name: _____  Date: _____

| CATEGORY | TOTAL | PROBLEMS | C | TLT |
|---|---|---|---|---|
| Order Entry-OSR Hard Copy | | | | |
| Order Entry-Customer Hard Copy | | | | |
| Order Entry-Customer (phone) | | | | |
| Order Entry-Outside Sales (phone) | | | | |
| Order Entry-Internal | | | | |
| Total Orders Entered | | | | |
| | | | | |
| Internal Order Admin. Task* (IO) | | | | |
| Not Real Time-One Time* (NR) | | | | |
| Stock Outs/Lost Sales* (LS) | | | | |
| Backorders Stock Item* (BS) | | | | |
| Substituted Item* (SI) | | | | |
| Go To Secondary Vendor* (SV) | | | | |
| | | | | |
| Incoming Inquiry-OSR/Customer | | | | |
| Incoming Inquiry-Other | | | | |
| Outgoing Phone-Customer | | | | |
| Outgoing Phone-Salesperson | | | | |
| Outgoing Phone-Internal | | | | |
| Outgoing Phone-Other | | | | |
| | | | | |
| RGA Credits | | | | |
| Other Credits | | | | |
| Outside Sales Order Error* (OSE) | | | | |
| Inside Sales Order Error* (ISE) | | | | |
| Product Dept. Order Error* (PE) | | | | |
| Distribution Center Order Error* (DE) | | | | |
| Customer Order Error* (CE) | | | | |
| Miscellaneous Order Error* (ME) | | | | |
| Quote Follow-up Over 48 hrs.* (QF) | | | | |
| Urgent Ship Request Denied* (RD) | | | | |
| | | | | |
| Research/Miscellaneous* (RM) | | | | |
| Weekly Expedite Report | | | | |
| Update Customer Profile | | | | |
| Process Credit Card | | | | |
| Sales Calls House Accounts | | | | |
| Shipping Confirmations | | | | |

assign activities—that is, asking a particular employee to perform specific activities using a checklist that serves as an official record that the activities have been assigned and received.

Once this is done, performance outcomes are not left to chance. Each individual discovers (and deserves to know) which activities management expects him or her to perform and how well (engaging employees is the third executing aspect to be discussed). Assigning activities in this way makes employees responsible for carrying out the assigned activities. This responsibility legitimately introduces employee accountability when management follows up (discussed in the next chapter) on how the assigned activities were performed.

## *Engaging Employees*

The third aspect of effective executing is management engaging employees to perform their activities ideally. As David Gergen rightly points out, "A leader's role is to raise people's aspirations for what they can become and to release their energies so they will try to get there."[2]

Engagement recognizes the critical importance of communicating to employees how they are to perform their assigned activities. Through measuring performance, management has quantitatively and qualitatively established how each activity can be ideally performed. Now it is the manager's role to engage each employee to "try to get there."

Obtaining ideal performance is not always easy or possible. Nevertheless, it is a manager's role to engage employees to make the effort, that is, to strive to perform their assigned activities ideally—perfectly.

Sadly many organizations do not practice employee engagement and never establish or communicate performance aspirations for their employees. In these situations, managers give their employees vague or indifferent performance expectations. It is only when something goes wrong are employees "engaged"—that is, put on the defensive to explain why an untoward performance outcome has occurred.

When management does not make it a practice to engage their employees in "trying to get there," it makes employees' work performance irrelevant and dampens their motivation to perform at a higher level. Consequently, employees dutifully carry out their assigned activities, unengaged and feeling unappreciated. They are left alone to wallow in mediocrity and sometimes failure, trapped in a management-created culture where ideal performance is not fostered.

Once, while I was practicing executing (and engaging employees to ideally perform their assigned activities), an employee approached me. With a smile on his face and an outstretched hand, he stated, "I have been with this company for over a year, and this is the first time a manager has treated me like a human being. Thank you! I'd like to shake your hand."

## *Empowering Employees*

Engaging employees—encouraging them to ideally carry out their assigned activities—has a galvanizing effect on performance. However, to sustain this effort requires that managers empower their employees, the fourth aspect of executing. Empowering employees is necessary because they will inevitably encounter problems when attempting to ideally perform their assigned activities. When problems are encountered, it will be necessary for the employee to take the initiative to address the problems so that hoped-for performance outcomes can be achieved.

Achieving satisfactory performance outcomes is execution's purpose. In a perfect world, it would be enough to develop a checklist and assign employees specific activities while engaging them to perform those activities ideally. But we don't live in a perfect world. Problems arise and these thwart ideal performance. Therefore, managers must empower employees to appropriately deal with the problems so that ideal performance outcomes can be obtained.

Empowerment recognizes employees' intimate knowledge of the activities they perform. This gives them a unique opportunity to aptly respond to problems, one not afforded to management. Consequently, it is imperative that management empower employees to take the appropriate action to address problems.

Empowering employees to take appropriate action assumes many forms. It may mean solving the problem, moderating the problem, or involving others better suited to solve the problem.

Empowerment invites employees to take the initiative. It asks them to participate in addressing the problems that compromise their performance. This invitation implies treating employees as valued colleagues. It signifies management and employees working together to improve performance.

For example, Toyota empowers auto assemblers to build quality automobiles. This entails giving them the power to stop the assembly line when problems arise. Although stopping the line is a very costly decision, Toyota employees have the power to take the appropriate action to address the problems they encounter.

It is imperative that the employees who actually perform the activities are empowered to address the problems they encounter, emboldening them to take the initiative to make the right things happen. As a result, empowered employees tackle problems, whereas apathetic employees accept them.

## The Practice of Executing

Now that we have discussed the four aspects of effective executing, it is time to begin practicing them. This initially happens (but never stops) when a manager hands an employee a checklist. In the ensuing conversation, the employee is formally assigned the activities listed on the checklist and engaged and empowered to ideally perform them.

The conversation goes something like this...

Good morning, Dan.

Today we are going to begin using a new management system designed especially for our Customer Service Department. Its purpose is to help me better manage how our department performs. However, this management system is not just for our department, as it will be implemented throughout the company's other departments as well. Soon all the company's managers will be using it to better manage their department's performance.

Better management will improve how our company performs. This will satisfy our customers, better our competiveness, and enable us to maintain if not grow sales. It will make us a stronger company, reducing our expenses and increasing our profits. It will also make your job more enjoyable and secure.

The system for managing produces specific results through fundamental management disciplines. For example, one specific result our department hopes to achieve is for customers to rate their service experience in the top 20 percent ratings range. Another hoped-for result is to use your and our other customer service representatives' time efficiently, where your measured performance efficiency is at least 85 percent.

Dan, here is one of the tools we'll ask you to use to help us improve our department's performance. This is a checklist that we have called a Daily Performance Report. Here is your copy [handing Dan a copy]. Starting this morning, I am going to ask you to use this.

Please enter your name and the date at the top of the page. Notice in the left-hand column is a list of activities. These are specific activities I am assigning you to carry out. You'll recognize most of these as they are activities that allow our department to successfully accomplish its aims. Let's review them, and I'll explain specifically what they are and how they are to be performed [going through the list].

Dan, do you understand the activities you have been assigned to perform? Great! The list of activities serves as a checklist. The checklist will be a reminder of the activities you have to perform and a record of the activities you have completed. It becomes a record of completed activities as you count them here in the column marked "Total." You do this throughout the day as an activity is completed. Also, Dan, at the end of the workday, please total the number of completed activities and place the respective total in the "Total" column.

In the next column, titled "Problems," I want you to document any problems you encounter. A problem is any situation that prevents you from carrying out an activity ideally—perfectly. For example, it's considered a problem when your time is wasted, when a customer is not pleased, or when company resources are wasted. Also, in documenting the problem, tell me what action, if any, you took to address the problem.

To help you document the problems, we have added two additional columns. In the next column, marked "C," we'll ask you to code the problems. For example, if a customer error caused the problem, code the problem a "CE." If outside sales caused the problem, then code the problem an "OSE." The codes are provided for you in parentheses next to the problems here in the left-hand column. Coding them will save you time in documenting the problems and help us organize and report them later.

In the column marked "TLT," record the total lost time, in minutes, that the problem caused you. This will help us quantify the problem and help us understand it more fully. It will also help us see how the problem impacted your performance.

I mentioned earlier that our department's planned aim is to utilize our customer service representatives 85 percent of the time. This will require us to measure how activities are performed. Let me explain how we will do this.

Here is a list of performance measures derived for each activity you perform [handing Dan the list]. A performance measure represents, in minutes, the ideal amount of time it should take you to complete an activity. Performance measures represent perfection and are used to compare your actual performance against the ideal, highlighting when problems occur.

Periodically throughout the day I'll take a look at your checklist and calculate your measured performance. This is done by multiplying the respective performance measure against the number of activities you have completed. This measurement will allow us to determine if ideal performance was achieved and, if not, to try to identify why.

For example, it should ideally take you three minutes to complete an Internal Order Entry. If you perform this activity in three minutes, your measured performance will be 100 percent. But let's say you run into a problem and it takes you six minutes to complete it. Then your measured performance will be only 50 percent.

Measuring your performance in this way highlights the problem. So whenever you run into problems, I am going to ask you to document what the problem was, including the additional three minutes it took you to resolve it. Identifying and documenting problems will enable us to understand the problem and take the appropriate action to address it. And when we do, it will not only make your job more efficient but also improve how we serve our customers—two of our departmental aims.

Dan, don't be alarmed if you cannot meet the performance ideal over short time periods. These measures are averages and may not average out in the short term but will over time. But on that point, if you can't meet the performance measure and you believe the reason is because the performance measure is not accurate, just let me know. We can re-measure the activity and confirm whether it is correct. If a performance measure is not accurate, we'll fix it—they are not set in concrete.

Dan, I want you to try to perform your assigned activities to the established performance measure. When you do, it indicates you performed the activities ideally. But please note that although we are striving to obtain perfect performance, we don't realistically expect it, not yet anyway. That is why we have established 85 percent as our measured performance aim and not 100 percent. Hopefully, as we identify and solve problems, we can aim for a higher performance outcome in the future.

So, Dan, when you encounter problems, don't feel you have to accept them. Instead, take the initiative to address them. Periodically, we will review what the appropriate action might be. But for now, don't accept problems as an inevitable part of your job but take action to solve them.

I'll stop by your desk every two hours to collect the information you have recorded. Each time I'll calculate your measured performance. This will give us a chance to discuss how you performed the activities. If your measured performance is not ideal, we can talk about the problems you have run into. Identifying the problems that make your job more difficult and inefficient and the customer's experience unsatisfactory is our focus. In doing so, we'll better understand the problems so that we can eliminate them. But we need your help to do that.

Dan, the information you report is very important. It will be used to assess how you perform and how we perform as a department. Each day it will be given to my manager. Each week the information is summarized and given to the company's VP and CEO. Therefore, the information must be accurate. Any fabrication of information is a serious matter that could jeopardize your future employment.

The management system we'll start using today is a tool to help us make the right things happen. We are committed to using it to solve problems and to support you in your efforts.

As I mentioned earlier, we will start this morning. Do you have any questions? Okay. I am sure you will once we begin. I'll let you get started. I'll see you in a couple of hours when I follow up on your performance results and see how you are doing.

## Conclusion

Employee conversations like this initiate executing. During the conversation, individual employees are given a checklist that assigns them specific activities to perform. Additionally, they are engaged and empowered to perform the activities ideally.

As mentioned earlier, executing is a pivotal discipline but it is not a conclusive one. It should come as no surprise that another management discipline is required to make certain that assigned activities have been performed ideally.

For it is only when managers practice following up will they discover how skillful their executing has been. The discovery process is categorical. It divides performance feedback into two categories: either the activities were performed ideally or not. This binary process occurs in the crucible of following up, the next learned discipline of management we now turn to.

## Chapter 5

# Following Up

*"You obtain the expected results when you inspect the means for acquiring them."*

—W. Edwards Deming

The stage is set. Through the learned disciplines of planning, organizing, measuring performance, and executing, management has commenced to make the right things happen. Now all that is left is for the main players (employees) to do their part. But is this really all that management requires?

While many managers do not get this far, there are still others who go no further. They stop at executing. They consider their job finished. They assume the assigned activities will be satisfactorily performed and completed. This is not management but make-believe. For activities are not always satisfactorily carried out, nor are they properly completed. Consequently, management must effectively follow up on the assigned activities to ensure that the expected performance outcomes have been achieved.

As author and consultant W. Edwards Deming observed, "You obtain the expected results when you inspect the means for acquiring them."[1] Following up accelerates making the right things happen. It entails managers periodically reviewing the results employees have obtained while carrying out their assigned activities.

As managers follow up (facilitated through executing), it produces four indispensable benefits. It creates actionable feedback, it aligns activities to produce expected results, it instills employee cooperation and fosters accountability, and it reinforces making the right things happen. Let's discuss how following up produces these four benefits.

## Create Actionable Feedback

Management follows up on assigned activities to ascertain how well the activities have been performed (later in this chapter, I'll show you how it's done) and to take action when performance is unsatisfactory. To rightly assess performance requires the manager to generate and collect actionable feedback (actionable feedback can also come from secondary sources, such as reports and records). Actionable feedback is performance information that is accurate, reliable, and timely; it is information that allows management to quantitatively and qualitatively assess performance and take the appropriate action to make the right things happen. Actionable feedback is critical in achieving successful performance outcomes. This principle was demonstrated in the fledgling aviation industry.

In aviation's early days, an airplane had two wings, two flight controls (a stick and rudder), and two flight instruments (a tachometer and compass). In favorable weather conditions, these two instruments were sufficient for the pilot to capably operate the aircraft, since he could observe the aircraft's wings in relation to the horizon and gauge the plane's distance from the ground.

However, in unfavorable weather conditions (fog, darkness, clouds, etc.), pilots could not visually orient their aircraft. In these conditions, a tachometer and compass were inadequate in giving pilots the feedback they required to pilot the aircraft, forcing them to rely on their instincts. Consequently, in bad weather, pilots depended on their feel for the aircraft's motion which was transmitted to the pilot's seat by centrifugal forces on his body as his aircraft turned, climbed or dove. Pilots using these physical cues for feedback were characterized as "flying by the seat of their pants." It was a dangerous practice.

For example, in 1918 the United States Postal Service inaugurated airmail service. Pilots were recruited and placed in unsophisticated aircraft to deliver airmail in all kinds of weather. These pilots, flying by the seat of their pants, suffered tragic consequences. From 1919 to 1926, accidents killed thirty-one of the first forty airmail pilots who entered the service.[2]

Not until 1937 did aviation technology catch up with the pilot's need for accurate, reliable, and timely feedback. By then, several crucial flight instruments were added to the cockpit. These included an artificial horizon, airspeed indicator, turn and bank indicator, and a vertical speed indicator. These instruments are found in modern aircraft today. They are designed to provide pilots actionable feedback so that they can skillfully operate their aircraft in all kinds of weather conditions. Actionable feedback is far superior to pilots having to fly by the seat of their pants.

Similarly, management depends on actionable feedback to achieve successful performance outcomes. For without actionable feedback, managers too are forced to depend on their instincts. Like early aviators, they must manage by the seat of their pants, relying on their impressions, intuition, appearances, feelings, and opinions. And like early aviators, managers' reliance on these ineffectual methods produces dismal results.

Let me give you an example of management flying by the seat of their pants. This case starkly demonstrates management's need for actionable feedback to effectively manage.

I was hired to improve a large industrial packaging company's performance and profitability. Despite its growing sales, the company struggled to perform effectively and efficiently. Consequently, its various departments needed more of everything (more employees, more overtime, more equipment, etc.), which eroded profitability.

This struggle to manage effectively was no less obvious than in the company's Inside Sales Department. In the past year, the department's annual budget had swelled by 43 percent (going from $490,000 to $700,000). From all outward appearances, this resource expenditure was necessary. Employees always seemed busy—often too busy—yet they failed to complete their assigned work activities. Management's response was to pour more resources into the department. But despite a 43 percent increase in expenditures, the department's employees still were not able to satisfactorily complete their assigned activities. Convinced that they lacked the necessary resources, the department's managers asked to hire even more employees.

Management's insistence that more employees were needed was an instinctual response based on appearances, opinions, and feelings. Unfortunately, this response was management's only recourse, since they were not practicing the learned disciplines of management.

However, this situation was soon remedied as the learned disciplines of management were custom tailored, deployed and practiced. For the first time, the department's managers had actionable feedback. To their dismay, it revealed that they had been flying by the seat of their pants—an inept and costly practice.

Through practicing following up, management generated and collected actionable feedback that depicted how activities were actually performed and reflected how resources were actually being used. Here is a feedback sampling indicating how six inside sales employees performed (measured in how efficiently their time was used performing their assigned activities) during the first week.

- Debbie's performance utilization measured 17 percent.

- Joan's performance utilization measured 23 percent.

- Meredith's performance utilization measured 25 percent.

- Mark's performance utilization measured 31 percent.
- David's performance utilization measured 35 percent.
- Mary's performance utilization measured 83 percent.

The department's combined employee performance utilization was a dismal 35 percent. This measure indicated that management did not need more employees but needed to better use the employees they had. This actionable feedback enabled and prompted management action that sought to determine why their employees' measured performance was so low and to take action to address it. Here is a partial description of what management had discovered.

Debbie's attitude and poor work habits explained her 17 percent performance utilization. Debbie considered herself a specialist in administering the company's equipment leasing business. However, this activity, unbeknownst to management, was not a full-time job. Despite this fact, Debbie had succeeded in appearing quite busy, carrying out her equipment leasing activities. Furthermore, she saw it beneath her status of "leasing administrator" to perform the department's other activities. Debbie's pretentions were now revealed through actionable feedback as management realized Debbie was underutilized.

Joan was not adequately trained, which explained her 23 percent performance utilization. Joan did not know how to use the new order entry software. Although she was initially trained on the software, the training did not stick. Afterward, she did not want to admit that she needed to be trained again. She feared her manager would conclude that she was not smart enough to do her job and would be fired. Rather than take that risk, she secretly asked her coworkers for help in doing her job (causing her coworkers' performance to suffer). For example, Joan resorted to handwriting orders and sneaking them out to the warehouse where she asked warehouse personnel to enter them into the computer for her.

Meredith's 25 percent performance utilization was explained because she performed activities not assigned on her activity checklist. Part of Meredith's assigned duties was to assist salespeople in administering their various customer accounts. However, these salespeople took advantage of Meredith's willingness to help by asking her to carry out personal activities. For example, salespeople asked her to schedule their dentist and doctor appointments, prepare expense reports, and run errands to the dry cleaner and florist under the guise it was freeing them up to sell.

Although Mark always appeared quite busy, his 31 percent performance utilization belied the fact that he did not have enough work to do. In following-up discussions, Mark admitted to his manager that he preferred acting busy to being busy. This was especially so if Mark did not like the work he was assigned to do. And the work he most disliked was making cold calls on inactive accounts. He was sure he'd be assigned this activity if he mentioned he did not have enough work to do. Instead, Mark chose to appear busy, pretending he had plenty to do until actionable feedback undid his charade.

David's 35 percent performance utilization was most perplexing to his manager. David always seemed unable to complete his work activities. This was reflected in the amount of overtime he worked, always the most among the department's employees. Yet actionable feedback showed his measured performance was very low. David's manager sought an explanation.

It was then that David admitted he intentionally put aside work during normal hours so that he could make more money working overtime. The company had a policy that every customer's order be entered into the computer system the day it was received. Taking advantage of this policy, David made it a practice to hide customer orders he received earlier in the day. When quitting time came, he had a ready-made excuse to work overtime. However, David's measured performance was diminished when he set aside and did not complete his activities. His measured performance was further reduced when additional overtime hours were added to the total hours he worked.

Surprisingly, Mary's measured performance utilization was 83 percent. Seemingly, this performance level was encouraging feedback. At least someone in the department was performing. But as the manager investigated how this performance came about, it only accentuated how ineptly the department was managed.

Mary was a dedicated employee committed to serving the customer. When her coworkers did not answer incoming customer phone calls, Mary picked up the phone. Over time, customers recognized Mary's dedication. When placing future orders, customers asked for Mary by name even though they had other assigned inside sales representatives. The others gladly let Mary do their jobs—who was to know? Also, Mary's coworkers counted on her help. Joan, for example, asked Mary to enter her handwritten orders. Mary ended up doing her work and the work of her coworkers as well. Amid the department's dysfunction, Mary soldiered on. Predictably, it was Mary's heavy workload that the department's managers pointed to in making the case to hire more employees.

Over the next three months, management used actionable feedback to make continuous improvements in employee performance. As a result, employees were properly trained, assigned enough work, and expected to satisfactorily complete their assigned work activities (and only their assigned activities). Improved performance produced many benefits. For example, the department's measured performance went from 35 percent to 71 percent. The department's customer service levels markedly improved. The department's employees were able to complete all their assigned activities. These improvements caused the department's operating costs to decline 30 percent and brought an end to the department's unceasing demand for more resources.

As this example demonstrates, flying by the seat of their pants is a feeble management practice. Instead, what management requires is actionable feedback. It takes accurate, reliable, and timely feedback to effectively assess performance and, when necessary, to use it to take appropriate action to make the right things happen.

Not only does management thrive on actionable feedback, but employees do too. Employees crave real feedback—not the superficial, patronizing kind that passes for most interactions between manager and employee, but feedback that is reliable, accurate, and timely.

This feedback is gathered in the immediacy of the moment when the work is being performed—not, as so often happens, when an employee's performance is evaluated every six to twelve months using the despised employee performance review. This review is despised for its hazy subjectivity and lack of timeliness. It is a performance review frequently based on a manager's recollections, opinions, and impressions. These make for partial and unreliable criteria to fairly assess an employee's work performance.

Feedback is meaningful and fair when it is gathered throughout the workday, where it is immediately understood and instantly applied to the activities being performed. This timeliness enables the manager to approve good performance and correct bad performance. Correcting bad performance happens right away when problems are identified. Consequently, performance is enhanced when problems are not allowed to persist, worsen, and spread but are decisively addressed in the immediacy of the moment.

But just as it is important to correct unsatisfactory work performance, it is equally important to affirm an employee's satisfactory work performance—for example, to reiterate that the employee performed his or her assigned activities excellently, as measured within the ideal performance parameters. This should also be done in the moment when the work activities are being performed, not six or twelve months later.

## Align Activities to Produce Results

Through executing, management has selected and assigned certain activities to be performed. It is expected that these activities will produce certain results. As management follows up, they have the opportunity to determine whether the expected results have been obtained. If not, management can align the right activities to produce the expected results.

Following up may reveal that the reason the expected results were not obtained is because the assigned activity was never completed. Or that it was not performed proficiently. Or that the assigned activity, even when skillfully performed, did not achieve the expected outcome, thus wasting resources. In these situations, following up gives management the chance to appropriately align activities to produce the expected performance outcomes.

For example, I was following up with a salesman on a Monday morning. The week before, he had been assigned twenty-five sales calls to perform. In reviewing the salesman's activity checklist, I noted that he had completed only twenty sales calls—five short of his assignment.

I asked, "Rob, why did you do only twenty sales calls last week and not twenty-five?"

He replied, "It rained on Thursday."

"What does that have to do with you doing twenty-five sales calls?" I asked.

"I don't do sales calls in the rain. I don't like getting my suit wet or my dress shoes splashed. I don't like having to get in and out of my car in the rain. So when it rained last Thursday, I did paperwork in my office," Rob explained.

"Rob, our company's success depends on executing crucial activities," I said. "One of these is making sales calls to sell our products and services. Last week you were asked to perform twenty-five sales calls. This was not an arbitrary number, nor was it optional. You could have had legitimate reasons for not doing twenty-five sales calls, but the fact that it rained last Thursday is not one of them. As a contrite Rob listened, I continued..."I suggest you buy an umbrella and galoshes—whatever it takes to do sales calls in the rain. What I don't expect is for you not to do your job. And your job is completing your assigned sales calls—rain or shine. Do you understand? Do you have any questions?"

He nodded his head.

"Good. I look forward to following up with you next week," I said.

As this example illustrates, aligning activities to produce the expected results came about through following up. In subsequent weekly follow-up sessions, Rob never failed to perform his assigned sales calls, even when it rained.

### Instill Cooperation and Foster Accountability

The third benefit to following up is that it instills and fosters employee and management cooperation and accountability. Employee cooperation is encouraged when manager and employee interact with each other when management frequently reviews and discusses how an employee performed. Employee cooperation and accountability is cultivated through these follow-up sessions. Following up compels manager-employee interaction, providing a ready-made context to develop a cooperative and accountable working relationship.

Management is a people-oriented profession requiring managers to work with and through people to make the right things happen. Following up establishes a platform where management can consistently interact with their employees, constructively supporting and encouraging the activities they carry out. This support is especially important when addressing problems that hinder an employee's performance. Management's involvement in solving problems not only encourages employee cooperation but also aids in employees' accountability as reasons for poor performance are removed.

Following up also instills *management* cooperation and fosters *management* accountability. Frequent follow-up sessions among management produces the same benefits that occur between employee and manager. This interaction develops strong working relationships among managers, enhancing cooperation and accountability.

## Reinforce Making the Right Things Happen

Finally, the fourth benefit to following up is that it reinforces making the right things happen. This occurs through repetition and reiteration, as achieving ideal performance is the focus of every follow-up session as management assesses whether ideal performance has been achieved. If it has not, management is prompted to take action to remedy the situation. These follow-up dynamics replicated over and over again reinforce making the right things happen.

An example where following up reinforced making the right things happen occurred while I was turning around a troubled auto parts manufacturer.

I followed up (soon after all the learned disciplines of management had been deployed) on an assembler I'll call Mike. Mike had been assigned the activity of assembling Chrysler automobile starters and had been performing this activity for the past two hours. I calculated Mike's performance over this time by multiplying the number of activities he had completed by their respective performance measures. Mike's performance measured 27 percent. I asked Mike what problems he had encountered that had caused him to lose 88 minutes during the previous 120-minute interval.

Mike responded, "The problem is the tensioner spring I am using. About a year ago, in a cost-cutting move, management decided to replace the green tensioner spring with a cheaper, generic version costing a penny less. The green spring they replaced was manufactured by Chrysler specifically for its starters and worked great. These cheaper, generic springs are junk and making them work is a headache. Let me show you what I mean."

Mike took a generic spring in hand and adjusted the spring's tension by pulling or compressing it using a pair of needle-nose pliers. Mike explained, "Each starter has two springs. I have to make these trial-and-error adjustments on both, trying to get the tension just right. Had I been using the green springs, I wouldn't have to do this. Instead, I would fit them into the starter and they worked perfectly every time.

"And that is the other problem. My adjustments don't always work perfectly, and I end up getting my starters rejected and returned to me. When this happens, I have to disassemble the starter, try and adjust the springs again, and then reassemble the unit. I then send it back down the line to be tested again, hoping it will pass. This generic spring is why I lose so much time."

Mike had been struggling with this problem for over a year. During that time, he had repeatedly tried to enlist management's help in solving the problem. However, his pleading for help had gone unheeded. Now here he was on a Monday morning with his needle-nose pliers in hand explaining how he lost eighty-eight minutes in the past two hours to a manager (me) he had only met the week before.

I documented the problem Mike had given me. Mike's explanation made sense. His measured performance was based on assembling starters, not adjusting springs and repairing rejected starters. I thanked him for the feedback. I told Mike I would do what I could to address the problem and I would get back to him soon.

Mike's follow-up session occurred just after 10:00 a.m., two hours into the shift. I wanted to use this follow-up session to reinforce making the right things happen. I wanted to use this opportunity to not only solve the problem but also to demonstrate to Mike and his coworkers management's commitment to support their work efforts in achieving ideal performance. Now if I could only deliver.

I phoned my purchasing manager and told him about my conversation with Mike. It was a situation he was all too familiar with (Mike had repeatedly asked him for green springs). I asked him how soon he could order the green springs and get them into the plant. Providentially, he replied that he happened to have a truck at the local vendor that moment picking up a previously placed parts order. He thought he could get the green springs added to the order and have them delivered to the plant by late morning. I asked him to go ahead and place the order.

When carrying out my afternoon follow-up session, I encountered a jubilant Mike. You'd have thought it was Christmas in July. He enthusiastically showed me his coveted green spring. "Look at what I've got!" he exclaimed, a big smile on his face. He then showed me how easy it was for him to assemble a Chrysler starter with green springs. It was a fact I already knew. Mike's measured performance had improved to 57 percent. Going down the line, I checked in with the line's test technician, collecting more feedback. The recorded starter failure rate had plummeted in the past two hours.

The next day's feedback showed that Mike's problem was solved. Mike's performance had dramatically improved, going from 27 percent to 82 percent. The tested starter failure rate improved as well, dropping to less than 1 percent (down from 24 percent). These results became the norm. Management, during following up, had reinforced making the right things happen.

## Practicalities of Following Up

Lastly, let's address how following up is practiced. The purpose of following up is to ascertain how effectively and efficiently assigned activities have been performed. To do this, management needs actionable feedback—that is, performance information that quantifiably and qualitatively enables management to assess how well assigned activities were performed.

Therefore, management's first step is to generate and collect actionable feedback. This effort is initiated through executing as employees are asked to document (on their activity checklist) what and how many activities were performed (when this performance data cannot be collected more easily elsewhere) and any problems that were encountered.

As management follows up on each employee, the employee's activity checklist continues to be used to generate and collect actionable feedback. It is used to calculate the employee's actual performance (multiplying the number of completed activities by their respective ideal performance measure), which is shared with the employee.

When ideal performance has been achieved, the employee's performance is commended. When ideal performance has not been achieved, it prompts a conversation between employee and manager. This discussion generates more actionable feedback, including what problems have been encountered, how costly were the problems (in lost time and wasted resources), and what action, if any, was taken to address the problems.

For instance, let's say during a two-hour period an employee completes twenty-four various activities that results in the employee's performance being measured at 50 percent. This feedback alerts manager and employee that the activities were not performed ideally and initiates and frames the conversation that follows. The conversation first conveys quantitatively (sixty minutes have been lost) that ideal performance has not been obtained. Second, it asks what problems have occurred that caused sixty minutes to be lost in a two-hour period. This question results in the identified problems being quantified (e.g., problem A cost twenty minutes, while problem B cost forty minutes) and documented so that it can be reported (more on real-time reporting in the next chapter) and appropriate action taken.

How frequently should following up be done? I have found that following up on employees in two- to three-hour periods works best. Most activities (those that can be completed in a matter of minutes) are completed during this time interval, permitting management to calculate actual performance. Also, more frequent following up makes collected feedback more relevant, since it is collected when the activities are actually being performed. This is especially important where a problem is encountered and its related details need to be recalled and explained so that appropriate action can be taken. A longer time interval often makes it more difficult to recollect what the problem was and to provide pertinent details. Longer intervals between follow-up sessions also allow problems to persist and negatively impact performance.

Where activities take longer to complete (measured in hours or days), following up on these activities can occur over longer intervals, but still limited to four- or five-hour periods for the reasons above. Even though an activity may not have been completed during this period (and actual performance cannot be calculated), a discussion can still take place about any problems that were encountered so that these problems can be immediately acted on. Also, this documented feedback can be used to explain unsatisfactory performance later when the activities are completed and actual performance is measured.

Follow-up sessions are intentionally brief, lasting no more than a few minutes (feedback organized on the checklist facilitates the session's brevity). The purpose of the session is to collect performance data, use it to assess how the assigned activities have been performed, and communicate this to the employee. Should a problem arise that will take more time to address, the manager schedules another more convenient time to do so, as the manager and employee often have other more pressing activities to carry out at the moment.

When communicating the performance results, it is important to encourage employee cooperation. This is especially important when ideal performance has not been obtained and a manager's natural response is to blame the employee. This rush to judgment must be avoided, as it inappropriately places the employee on the defensive, creating an adversarial relationship instead of a cooperative one.

As we have already discussed, performance measurement can be uncomfortable. This discomfort is exaggerated when an employee's performance is not ideal. This not only increases the pressure on an employee to perform but also intensifies the employee's frustration and insecurities. Consequently, management must deal with these follow-up dynamics tactfully to create a cooperative work environment, since most employees are trying to do their best in carrying out their assigned activities.

Therefore, during the follow-up sessions, management must reassure employees that the purpose of the session is not to manipulate, criticize, and callously control an employee's performance but to constructively identify and address the problems that affect an employee's performance. When employees discover that management's focus is not necessarily on them but on the problems they encounter, it causes the tension to subside. In time, as management creates a cooperative, collaborative work environment, employees willingly participate in the follow-up process.

Similarly, following up can be uncomfortable for a manager whose performance is assessed. Following up reinforces management making the right things happen and does not accept a manager's inaction, missteps, and half measures. But just as an employee needs reassuring during follow-up, so too does management. Therefore, the management follow-up session focus is the same—to identify and solve problems.

### Typical Following-Up Scenarios

When practicing following up, management will typically encounter five different scenarios, each requiring a particular response.

In the first follow-up scenario, ideal performance is achieved. When this happens, it is appropriate, even necessary, for the manager to acknowledge and praise the employee for a job well done. This positive management interaction may very well be the first time (but hopefully not the last time) the employee is recognized for doing an excellent job.

As already noted, it is a deeply felt human need to have one's work acknowledged and appreciated. For instance, studies have shown that people are more motivated by praise and appreciation than by a raise in pay or a promotion. Consequently, appreciation for a job well done is a natural by-product of following up.

I'll never forget the look on an employee's face, one of shock and delight, as the company's CEO stopped by his workstation and said, "John, I saw your last week's performance results—keep up the great work!" This was the first positive interaction John had ever had with the company's CEO (or any other company executive for that matter). In the CEO's defense, this was the first time he had actionable feedback to praise his employee's performance.

News of the CEO's visit and his talk with John spread quickly throughout the department and company. This interaction created a lasting and positive impression—one that was sustained as management frequently followed up and regularly communicated praise to deserving employees.

A second more common follow-up scenario is when an employee is assigned work activities but was not able to perform them ideally. When a manager communicates this to the employee, the employee shares several documented problems that were encountered. The employee also documents how much time each problem cost and the action taken to address them.

The feedback seemingly documents and creditably explains the problems. Also, the action the employee took to address the problems (sometimes the only action available to an employee is to document the problem) was satisfactory.

Management's response is to thank the employee for the valuable feedback. When possible, the manager explains the action that will be taken to address the documented problems (action within or outside the department or both).

The employee is praised for a job well done (except in those cases where the encountered problems were the employee's own making). Although the performance ideal was not achieved, the employee did all that could reasonably be expected.

A variation on this second example would be when the employee correctly documents the encountered problems but took the wrong approach in responding to the problems. This situation allows the manager to intervene, training the employee to appropriately respond to the problems.

In a third follow-up scenario, the employee does not achieve ideal performance. The employee documents the problems but not creditably. For instance, the problems' impact is exaggerated or understated and misses the mark. In this situation, the manager helps the employee to better analyze and think through the problems' implications. This may include reviewing how the activities should be performed or explaining how to identify and document problems.

In a fourth follow-up scenario, the employee claims he or she has no idea why the performance ideal was not met. As far as the employee is concerned, everything went normally without any problems. As in the previous scenario, this gives the manager the opportunity to review and help the employee better understand that "normal" may not be the ideal.

Perhaps the problem unknowingly rests with the employee. Perhaps the employee is not fully trained or lacks the basic skills to perform the job. Perhaps one or more performance measures are not accurate. Perhaps it was a period where measured performance did not represent the average but will over time. Over time, each of these possibilities will sort themselves out as management continually assesses performance and identifies and acts on the problem source.

The fifth and final follow-up scenario is the most challenging. It's where the employee does not obtain the performance ideal and, in response, falsely fabricates information to appease management.

Unengaged, uncooperative, and feeling threatened, this employee has decided to simply go through the motions in filling out the checklist. Perhaps the employee is trying to hide poor performance issues. Perhaps the employee feels entitled to his or her job and isn't concerned with their performance.

Overcoming this employee's attitude is a daunting challenge. Sometimes the employee can be reformed, especially when the employee sees the positive results of management's efforts. Meanwhile, an employee is warned not to provide false information on his or her checklist and encouraged to participate in the process.

The prospect of this employee's future employment is doubtful. Without an improved attitude, including a willingness to cooperate with management, this employee's continued presence would allow the wrong things to happen.

## Conclusion

Following up enables management to produce actionable feedback, assess performance, identify and solve problems, align activities to produce expected results, and instill employee and management cooperation and accountability. Following up is a decisive management practice that reinforces making the right things happen.

The practice of following up has generated and collected actionable feedback. In the next chapter, we will take this feedback and multiply its efficacy to make the right things happen through the practice of real-time reporting.

## Chapter 6

# Real-Time Reporting

> For the great majority of mankind are satisfied with appearance, as though they were realities and are often more influenced by the things that seem than by those that are.
> —Machiavelli

In November 1944, the US Third Army was engaged in a war of attrition against stiffening German resistance as the Allies slogged east through France toward Germany. Commanding the Third Army was a three-star general named George S. Patton, who was regarded as the Allies' most capable field commander.

As Patton reviewed the latest casualty reports, he noticed a distressing statistic. Nonbattle casualties were rising to alarming numbers: 3,000 cases of trench foot in one division alone (at one point, more than 18,000 of Patton's 220,000 troops were down with trench foot and other related ailments). Trench foot was becoming a greater threat to his men than the Germans they were fighting.

A debilitating foot fungus, trench foot was a common plight among US infantrymen. Wearing inadequate boots, the men were forced to hunker down in cold, wet trenches, their feet vulnerable to infection. As the infection worsened, the soldiers became immobile, rendering them noncombatant.

Patton didn't understand why so many of his men were falling prey to this medical condition. After all, the army had an effective policy to prevent trench foot. Each infantryman was supposed to be issued two pairs of wool socks. While wearing one pair, the soldier could clean and dry the second pair, changing between the two pairs as necessary. Patton went to the front lines to investigate what the problem might be.

He was shocked by what he found. His men had been issued only one pair of wool socks. It was this one pair they wore constantly in the winter cold and mud-filled trenches. Army policy has been entirely ignored, and Patton was determined to find out why.

He first discovered it was not because of a sock shortage. There was an almost inexhaustible supply of wool socks in the nearby military depots. Instead, he found they were not passed out to the men who desperately needed them. With this feedback, Patton took action to solve the problem.

He ordered two pairs of socks to be issued to each infantryman. To make sure this happened, he organized the distribution. When the men received their daily hot meal, they also received a fresh pair of socks. He ordered his men to change out of their wet socks and into dry ones at least once a day. He assigned the men's officers the task of personally inspecting their men's feet to make sure the men had changed their socks. He threatened to relieve any commander who did not follow through on his orders. He also alerted the army quartermasters (the army branch responsible for material supply) to keep his men supplied with socks. Patton's actions caused trench foot casualties to plummet, enabling his soldiers to focus on fighting the enemy.[1]

In this example, Patton used actionable feedback he gathered from real-time reporting (casualty reports) to make follow-up visits to the front lines. This performance information bridged the gulf between frontline troops and a three-star general, allowing him to identify problems and to take action to solve them. Afterward, real-time reporting was used to confirm that the problem was solved and to monitor whether it remained so.

As we learned in the previous chapter, management requires reliable, timely, and accurate performance information to effectively follow up on assigned activities. This actionable feedback must now be disseminated throughout the organization so that management at all levels can assess performance outcomes and take action to make the right things happen. The practice of real-time reporting ensures that performance information is shared throughout the organization.

There is nothing like the sheer power of real-time reported feedback to scrub away layers of ignorance, inaction, incompetence, confusion, concealment, and contradiction. Effective managers harness this power. They use real-time reported feedback to avoid the trap observed by the Italian political theorist Machiavelli, who said, "For the great majority of mankind are satisfied with appearance, as though they were realities and are often more influenced by the things that seem than by those that are."[2]

Successful managers avoid relying on appearances. Instead, they use real-time reported performance information to discern reality, enabling them to take action on the things that are.

## Real-Time Reporting Essentials

Authentic real-time reporting emerges through management follow-up. During follow-up, management generates and gathers actionable feedback that depicts how activities were performed. This reported feedback is real. It comes from those who are actually performing or managing the activities. Their intimate familiarity (their "eye-witness testimony," as it were) with the activities they perform makes the feedback credible, factual, and compelling.

Real-time reporting is also timely. Its timeliness arises from being gathered in the moment when the activity is being performed and then promptly shared with employees and management. It is not reconstructed information put together after the fact. It is not historic information collected long after the activities have happened. It is not projected information, forecasting what might happen. Instead, real-time performance information is a few minutes to a few hours old. And its power is multiplied when immediately shared throughout the organization.

## Real-Time Reporting Is Not Accounting Information

Before we discuss how real-time reporting is practiced, a distinction needs to be drawn between it and accounting information. This is an important distinction because many companies imprudently use accounting information to manage performance. This practice is ill advised, for accounting information does not adequately give management the information they need to manage performance in two primary ways.

First, accounting information was never intended to be used to manage performance. Accounting was originally practiced for financial planning and later for tax compliance. Accounting information (reported through income statements, balance sheets, and other reports) is not designed to manage performance—that is, to manage how essential activities are effectively and efficiently carried out.

Accounting information measures profits and losses, various costs, inventory turns, return on investment, and so on. Although these are important financial determinants, they are inadequate for managing performance.

For instance, accounting reports measure profit, but this measure is one-dimensional. It fails to give management the information they need to produce a profit. Profits result when crucial activities are effectively managed, maximizing resources and results. It is this performance information—not accounting information—that enables a manager to effectively manage activities.

Second, accounting information is historic information. It is a look back in time, usually the previous month's financial results. This monthly look back is fine for financial planning but ruinous for managing performance.

Relying on accounting information to manage performance

lulls management into inaction as they wait to receive monthly reported financial results. If the reported results do not meet expectations, a scramble ensues to discover why. Now management is forced to act more like detectives than managers. They must attempt to collect clues (days to weeks old) to explain the poor results. If they are successful, this information can be used to address problems that have, over the intervening time, been allowed to diminish performance outcomes.

Accounting information is at best a shadow that vaguely reflects how an organization performed. Relying on shadows to manage performance is ineffective. Instead, effective management thrives on timely, dedicated performance information. As this information is dispersed (through real-time reporting), it provides management with a powerful and effective alternative to accounting information.

## The Six Features of Real-Time Reporting

Real-time reporting has six features that make management more effective:

1. Real-time reporting distributes performance information.

2. Real-time reporting structures follow-up meetings.

3. Real-time reporting perpetuates ideal performance.

4. Real-time reporting links the practice of the learned disciplines of management.

5. Real-time reporting identifies best practices.

6. Real-time reporting facilitates problem solving.

Let's see how these real-time reporting features work.

## *Real-Time Reporting Distributes Performance Information*

A treasure trove of performance information is generated and collected through practicing the learned disciplines of management. In order to unleash this feedback's potential, it must be shared throughout the organization. To accomplish this, management practices real-time reporting; that is, management takes the collected performance information and effectively conveys it to those who can use it to make the right things happen.

Real-time reporting begins when following up with employees. During the follow-up sessions, the manager collects, measures, and documents each employee's performance. This performance information is shared with the employee.

During this interaction, if the reported performance is not ideal, additional feedback is gathered in an attempt to explain why. This feedback, along with the other performance information, is now arranged so that it can be reported throughout the organization on a daily and weekly basis. Here's how this is done.

Let's say a manager has ten employees. During the workday, he follows up on each employee every two hours, or four times per day. This represents forty follow-up sessions where real-time performance information has been collected. This includes, for example, how many assigned activities each employee completed and measures indicating how well the activities were performed, as well as the number of problems encountered.

Much of this information has been generated by the employees themselves on their activity checklists (see the Daily Performance Report example in chapter four). Additional performance information is generated from outside sources such as payroll documents, phone records, specialized reports, and so on. The manager also adds to the collected feedback as he or she interacts with employees regarding the problems the employees encountered.

This is a lot of information. To make the information more concise, usable, and portable, it is summarized and reported daily and weekly on a report titled the "Daily Performance Summary" (shown on next page).

The Daily Performance Summary example includes such information as the number of employees assigned to the department, the total number of employee hours planned (actual and overtime), the combined department's measured performance (stated as Performance Utilization %), each employee's measured performance (ISR: Name Performance Utilization %), the number of various activities that were completed, documented problems (problem details are provided separately on an attached report), and specific performance ratios.

For example, the performance ratio "Customer Survey Response Rating Avg." was added to this Daily Performance Summary. This ratio reported how surveyed customers rated the service they were provided.

Ratios like this (appendix B lists some other typical departmental ratios) are often added to the Daily Performance Summary, expanding reported performance information to enrich management's perspective.

When each workday concludes, the day's performance data (combined from the Daily Performance Reports or activity checklists) is added to the Daily Performance Summary. When the week concludes, each day's data is tallied in the far right column marked "Total." This total summarizes performance data for the week.

Real-time performance information is summarized one more time on a report titled "Weekly Performance Summary" (shown on page 142).

The Weekly Performance Summary summarizes and compares the department's weekly performance. Each week's performance is placed in a column next to the preceding week's performance. Over time (weekly, monthly, quarterly and yearly), this provides a comparative look at each week's

# INSIDE SALES DEPARTMENT
# DAILY PERFORMANCE SUMMARY

Week Ending: _____

| CATEGORY | Mon. | Tue. | Wed. | Thur. | Fri. | Sat. | Total |
|---|---|---|---|---|---|---|---|
| Total Number of Employees Assigned | | | | | | | |
| Total Employee Regular Hours Planned | | | | | | | |
| Total Employee Overtime Hours Planned | | | | | | | |
| Total Employee Regular Hours Actual | | | | | | | |
| Total Employee Overtime Hours Actual | | | | | | | |
| Departmental Performance Utilization % | | | | | | | |
| ISR: Name    Performance Utilization % | | | | | | | |
| ISR: Name    Performance Utilization % | | | | | | | |
| ISR: Name    Performance Utilization % | | | | | | | |
| ISR: Name    Performance Utilization % | | | | | | | |
| ISR: Name    Performance Utilization % | | | | | | | |
| ISR: Name    Performance Utilization % | | | | | | | |
| ISR: Name    Performance Utilization % | | | | | | | |
| | | | | | | | |
| Orders Processed-Hard Copy | | | | | | | |
| Orders Processed-Phone | | | | | | | |
| Total Orders Processed | | | | | | | |
| Average Order Dollar Amount $ | | | | | | | |
| Total Add-on Sales Dollars $ | | | | | | | |
| Total Existing Customer Sales Calls | | | | | | | |
| Total Existing Customer Sales Dollars $ | | | | | | | |
| Total New Customer Sales Calls | | | | | | | |
| Total New Customer Sales Dollars $ | | | | | | | |
| Total Quotes Processed | | | | | | | |
| Total Sample Requests Processed | | | | | | | |
| Total Stock Keeping Agreements Processed | | | | | | | |
| Total Inquiries Processed | | | | | | | |
| Total Items Stocked Out-Lost Sale | | | | | | | |
| Total Items Stocked Out-Substituted Item | | | | | | | |
| Total Returned Goods/Credits Processed | | | | | | | |
| Total Number of Problems Identified | | | | | | | |
| Total Number of Problems Hours Lost | | | | | | | |

## INSIDE SALES DEPARTMENT
## WEEKLY PERFORMANCE SUMMARY

| Category                                  Week Ending ▶ | | | | | | |
|---|---|---|---|---|---|---|
| Total Number of Persons | | | | | | |
| Total Employee Regular Hours Planned | | | | | | |
| Total Employee Overtime Hours Planned | | | | | | |
| Total Employee Regular Hours Actual | | | | | | |
| Total Employee Overtime Hours Actual | | | | | | |
| Departmental Performance Utilization % | | | | | | |
| ISR: Name     Performance Utilization % | | | | | | |
| ISR: Name     Performance Utilization % | | | | | | |
| ISR: Name     Performance Utilization % | | | | | | |
| ISR: Name     Performance Utilization % | | | | | | |
| ISR: Name     Performance Utilization % | | | | | | |
| ISR: Name     Performance Utilization % | | | | | | |
| ISR: Name     Performance Utilization % | | | | | | |
| | | | | | | |
| Orders Processed-Hard Copy | | | | | | |
| Orders Processed-Phone | | | | | | |
| Total Orders Processed | | | | | | |
| Average Order Dollar Amount $ | | | | | | |
| Total Add-on Sales Dollars $ | | | | | | |
| Total Existing Customer Sales Calls | | | | | | |
| Total Existing Customer Sales Dollars $ | | | | | | |
| Total New Customer Sales Calls | | | | | | |
| Total New Customer Sales Dollars $ | | | | | | |
| Total Quotes Processed | | | | | | |
| Total Sample Requests Processed | | | | | | |
| Total Stock Keeping Agreements Processed | | | | | | |
| Total Inquiries Processed | | | | | | |
| Total Items Stocked Out-Lost Sale | | | | | | |
| Total Items Stocked Out-Substituted Item | | | | | | |
| Total Returned Goods/Credits Processed | | | | | | |
| Total Number of Problems Identified | | | | | | |
| Total Number of Problems Hours Lost | | | | | | |
| Customer Survey Response Rating Avg. | | | | | | |

performance results, trends, and key performance indicators.

Documentation supporting the Daily Performance Summary and Weekly Performance Summary is provided through supporting Daily Performance Reports and the department manager's follow-up notes.

The Daily Performance Summary and Weekly Performance Summary are used to disseminate performance information throughout the organization. This is done in structured meetings, first with each employee, next with all of the department's employees, third with middle management, and finally with executive management.

## *Real-Time Reporting Structures Follow-up Meetings*

The second feature of real-time reporting is the structured follow-up meeting. In these meetings, performance information is shared with the appropriate party through the Daily Performance Summary and the Weekly Performance Summary.

The first structured meetings are between managers and their individual employees. Although these employees have been given feedback during frequent follow-up sessions, they have yet to receive a daily and weekly summary of their performance. This information has been compiled on the Daily Performance Summary.

On a daily basis (typically when the manager is already following up with each employee), the information contained in the Daily Performance Summary is shared. The previous day's performance feedback includes an individual employee's performance results, as well as collective performance information that summarizes how the department performed. The previous week's individual and department performance results are also shared weekly with employees during a second structured meeting.

In addition to structured meetings, individual and collective performance feedback is shared with employees by posting the Daily Performance Summary within the department. This posting allows all of the department's employees to see how their performance compares to their coworkers and often leads to elevated performance as lagging employees strive to perform comparably.

The department manager will later use the Daily Performance Summary in the third structured meeting, reporting the department's daily performance to his boss—usually a midlevel manager. Up until now, the department manager's focus has been on following up and managing his or her employees' performance. In this meeting, the department manager's performance is assessed and managed.

This is done as the department manager communicates the real-time performance information contained in the Daily Performance Summary. This report details individual and collective performance, which reflects how well the department has been managed. The meeting also has as its focus any documented problems that have negatively impacted performance. These problems are discussed to determine if the appropriate action has been taken to solve them.

The fourth and final structured meeting is between the midlevel manager and the manager's boss, usually a vice president or CEO (depending on how managerially flat the organization is). During the meeting, the department's real-time performance information from the previous weeks (contained on the Weekly Performance Summary) is presented to executive management. This shared feedback gives executive management the opportunity to note how well the department performed and to assess how effectively it was managed by the department manager and the manager's boss.

It is instructive for middle and executive management to receive real-time performance information. Often, these managers are isolated from the employees and the activities they perform. Consequently, the further removed from the activities, the less middle and executive management know about what satisfactory performance requires.

For these managers, real-time reported information bridges

this gap, giving them insight into the realities (especially the problems) their employees and managers face. The sharing of accurate, reliable, and timely feedback (that had rarely left the immediate area) is now commonly shared with management at all levels of the organization. Its dissemination makes little-known performance issues everybody's issues as previously insulated managers are engaged in making the right things happen.

These structured follow-up meetings are concise, taking a few minutes with employees and about fifteen minutes with managers. The meeting's focus is on improving performance. Should issues arise during the meeting that require more time to address, another lengthier meeting is scheduled. This meeting should be held at a convenient time so that the issues can be fully explored and appropriately addressed. This avoids employees and managers being drawn into a lengthy discussion they are not prepared to have while their pending work responsibilities go unattended.

When I propose meeting on a daily and weekly basis, I am not suggesting another pointless meeting. Nor am I equating a brief meeting with a superficial one. Instead, through the exchange of real-time performance information, managers are able to effectively focus on improving performance. This is done as management rigorously uses quantifiable and qualitative feedback to determine if the organization has achieved its aims. As performance improves, meeting daily may not be necessary, and the meeting can be held less frequently. However, until performance outcomes reach a satisfactory level, the meeting frequency should continue on a daily and weekly basis.

### *Real-Time Reporting Perpetuates Ideal Performance*

Real-time reporting perpetuates ideal performance; this is its third feature. Perpetuating ideal performance is crucial, for it creates an organizational culture of performance excellence. Promoting and preserving ideal performance is especially important in organizations that have not consistently practiced the learned disciplines of management and have allowed the wrong things to happen. Over time, these organizations have formed a culture in which second-rate performance is commonplace. Changing this culture is as necessary as it is difficult.

Real-time reporting can aid in establishing and perpetuating a culture of excellent performance. Real-time reporting makes ideal performance outcomes the organization's constant and inescapable focus. This focus impacts how activities are carried out as individuals and managers are given real-time performance information assessing whether they have achieved ideal performance. Over time, this focus eventually makes ideal performance routine.

For instance, let's say a manager follows up on an employee and discovers the employee's measured performance is only 40 percent. The first thing the manager does is share this feedback with the employee. This in turn prompts a discussion: What problems occurred that caused a 60 percent loss in performance? The discussion reveals the employee does not know how to perform several activities. The manager now recognizes the problem and determines that the employee needs to be trained. It is expected that the manager will take the appropriate action to achieve ideal performance.

But what if, for whatever reason, the manager does not train the employee and continues to allow the wrong things to happen? The untrained employee persists in poorly performing his or her assigned activities and, in follow-up after follow-up, the employee's measured performance remains at 40 percent.

When the department manager meets with his or her boss to go over the department's results, the department manager reports that an employee's measured performance was only 40 percent. The department manager explains the reason for the lost time is because the employee was not adequately trained to do his or her job. The manager acknowledges he or she did not get around to training the employee.

In the unlikely event that the department manager's boss accepts this response, the reported problem does not go away. Poor performance in fact continues to be measured and reported during each follow-up session. Now the midlevel manager must report this performance outcome to his or her boss, usually a company executive, acknowledging that not only did the department manager not take action to train the employee but also that he or she did not take the appropriate action.

As this instance illustrates, real-time reporting highlights mediocre results and the ineffective performance that caused these results. As real-time performance information is exchanged, the responsibility (and opportunity) to achieve ideal performance spreads through the management ranks, resting finally with executive management. If a manager and midlevel manager fail to make the right things happen, it is executive management that must take action to achieve ideal performance, holding accountable those managers who have allowed the wrong things to happen.

Over time, ideal performance is perpetuated as performance outcomes are constantly reported and unsatisfactory outcomes are acted on. Crucially, the reporting of real-time performance information is not an academic exercise in which bad performance and the problems that caused it are presented and discussed but nothing is done about it. This response only perpetuates mediocre performance, causing an organization's aims to go unrealized. Instead, practicing real-time reporting instills accountability and promotes action. It is a discipline that impacts how an organization performs and perpetuates a culture where ideal performance is continually assessed and constantly pursued.

For example, I once consulted a manager we'll call Fred. After his first day of using the learned disciplines of management, Fred reported that his department performance measured only 35 percent. He had documented a partial list of problems his employees had encountered. It was a partial list because Fred did not fully account for his department's lost time.

In the early stages of practicing the learned disciplines of management, this is not uncommon. There is often a learning curve for managers unaccustomed to using real-time performance information to identify and address problems. In time, most managers learn to do this. This was our expectation for Fred.

Fred's first week trying to use the real-time reported information came to a close. But he had yet to make any progress in improving his department's performance—it remained around 35 percent. However, Fred did improve in identifying the problems his department encountered.

What was most remarkable about Fred's efforts was not his growing ability to identify problems but his inability to solve them. In Fred's real-time reporting, the section marked "Action Taken" was blank (except where his employees took action).

As the weeks passed, Fred's management results had reached a plateau. His department's measured performance went up slightly to 38 percent. Despite constant coaching and intense training, Fred's reported "Action Taken" remained inexplicably nonexistent.

As time passed, it became obvious what the problem was. It was Fred. Although he was given the tools to manage his department, he did not have the ability to use them to solve problems. As a result, he was fired, having lost a management position he had held for seven years. A short time later, his replacement was able to solve many of the problems Fred had identified, causing the department's performance to improve to 80 percent.

Sadly, Fred's experience is not an isolated one. Giving managers the tools they need to effectively do their job, training them in how to use the tools, and supporting them in their use are necessary first steps. But the learned disciplines of management alone cannot solve problems. It takes a manager who is able to use the tools to not only report the problems but also, more importantly, to solve them. When a "manager" lacks this ability, real-time reporting makes it obvious, providing the necessary feedback to hold them accountable. In this case, real-time reporting showed that Fred was unable to make the right things happen, which resulted in the action of replacing him with a manager who could.

## *Real-Time Reporting Links the Practice of the Learned Disciplines of Management*

Real-time reporting links the practice of the seven learned disciplines of management. This is the fourth feature. Linking the practice of these disciplines is crucial. For it is only when each individual discipline is practiced that a powerful, self-reinforcing management system for making the right things happen is formed. The formation (and constant execution) of this management system will not happen unless safeguards are put into place to reinforce its practice.

Bringing about lasting organizational change is difficult. For instance, management introduces a new program or initiative with great fanfare only to revisit it six months later and discover that it is no longer being practiced. The reason is inertia, which causes even the best of ideas to lose momentum and eventually fall out of practice. Left unchecked, change becomes impossible as an organization inevitably reverts to its old ways of doing things, thus producing the same unsatisfactory results that management tried to avoid. Consequently, for management to bring about lasting change, deterrents must be put into place to combat organizational inertia.

To ensure that the learned disciplines of management are universally assimilated and effectively practiced, they must be linked, which is what real-time reporting does. Such linkages safeguard their constant and consistent practice and result in management making the right things happen. Ultimately, the organization's CEO anchors this linkage. As long as the CEO insists that the management team practice the learned disciplines, they will continue to be used.

Although real-time reporting is the final, most obvious

link in ensuring the learned disciplines are systematically practiced, it is not the only one. Other linkages are also in place to choreograph the effective fulfillment of the management disciplines. Linked to management's practice of execution are the disciplines of planning, organizing, and measuring performance. If these disciplines are not successfully carried out, effective execution is not possible. Linked to execution is following up. If management does successfully execute, effective follow-up cannot be done. Linked to following up is real-time reporting. Unless management has followed up and generated and collected real-time performance information, real-time reporting cannot be practiced (for there is no real-time performance information to convey).

When this happens, the CEO is the last to know. In the CEO's meeting to review the previous week's real-time performance information, the CEO will discover there is none to receive. If the CEO is committed to practicing the learned disciplines of management, this will be the last time this happens.

I recall an incident where I had deployed the learned disciplines of management in an Engineering Department. For several weeks, the department's manager had dutifully practiced the management disciplines, allowing him to complete the Engineering Daily Performance Summary. It was this report he shared in a daily meeting with his boss—a vice president.

However, one day we went into the daily management meeting and the engineering manager sheepishly presented his Engineering Daily Performance Summary. It was blank. The vice president looked at the blank page with dismay and asked the engineering manager, "What is this?"

Meekly and apologetically, the manager responded that he did not get around to following up on his employees the previous day and therefore had no real-time performance information to report.

"We have three problems," the vice president said. "One problem is that you did not do your job yesterday. This is evidenced by your blank report. The second problem will happen next week when I have to report to the CEO your incomplete report. I can tell you he will not be happy with you or me. The third problem and perhaps the most troubling is how your negligence has impacted our employees.

"I have watched with interest as they have responded to our management initiatives. Day after day, they have provided us with real-time performance information, including a host of identified problems. Because of their input, we have been making steady progress in improving your department's performance. No doubt, they gathered real-time performance information yesterday, information you did not bother to collect. What message does that send to them about our stated commitment to make the right things happen? Let's conclude this meeting. I expect you to do two things, which are not optional. First, go back and reconstruct, as best you can, yesterday's real-time performance results. Second, don't let this happen again."

As this example illustrates, linking the practice of the learned disciplines through real-time reporting makes it obvious whether they are actually carried out. With this link in place, it is not uncommon for me to visit a former client several years after the learned disciplines of management have first been deployed to discover that they are still being faithfully and effectively practiced.

But organizational inertia is ever present. Even in organizations that have seen performance dramatically improve through practicing the learned disciplines of management, I am often asked when this practice can end. These managers and employees believe they have satisfied all the requirements necessary for excellent performance and that they no longer need to practice the learned disciplines of management.

They assume that old problems will not return and new problems will not arise. Meanwhile, they discount how practicing the learned disciplines of management has sustained their successful performance.

Fortunately, real-time reporting serves as a ready antidote, keeping inertia at bay. It links the practice of the seven learned disciplines of management, ensuring that the right things happen.

## *Real-Time Reporting Identifies Best Practices*

Real-time reporting helps management to identify (and implement) best practices—the fifth feature. Real-time performance information depicts individual employee and manager performance. When these performance results are compared, it highlights discrepancies in performance outcomes. The ability to achieve ideal performance often indicates the absence of problems, but it can also indicate the use of best practices. Best practices produce the best performance outcomes. Once these are identified, the best practices can be replicated and broadly implemented to ideally carry out the assigned activities.

Let's say there are two employees, Bob and Lorie, who perform the same activity. Bob's performance is reported at 85 percent, whereas Lories' performance is reported at 65 percent. The reported performance disparity gives management the opportunity to uncover what Bob is doing that Lorie is not. Absent problems, Bob has obviously found ways to perform the activities more effectively and efficiently. Identifying these best practices allows management to replicate them. When these best practices are implemented, performance is generally improved.

Real-time reporting also reinforces best practice development. When management identifies best practices, it also recognizes those who have taken the initiative to develop them. This recognition demonstrates an appreciation for an employee's initiative and resourcefulness in developing the best practices and fosters an environment where their development is valued and encouraged.

## *Real-Time Reporting Facilitates Problem Solving*

Finally, the sixth feature of real-time reporting is its ability to facilitate problem solving. This is explored in greater depth in the next chapter as we take up the last learned discipline of management.

## Conclusion

Actual, timely, and accurate performance feedback is essential for excellent performance outcomes. Through the practice of real-time reporting, performance information is disseminated throughout the organization; apprising everyone, everywhere of individual and collective performance outcomes so that they can participate in making the right things happen.

## Chapter 7

# Problem Solving

We shall be better, braver, and more active men if we believe it right to look for what we do not know.

—Socrates

Why is it that over 38,000 US businesses go bankrupt each year?[1] Obviously, this was not management's aim or desired end. Instead, management's aims were thwarted when they allowed the wrong things to happen. These wrong things are problems that have gone unrecognized and unresolved. Left unchecked, the problems were allowed to persist, deepen, and multiply, degrading performance, squandering resources, and eliminating profits.

Management's unwillingness or inability to solve systemic problems has inevitable and sobering consequences. The 38,000 businesses that fail annually, not to mention the countless other businesses that wallow in mediocrity, are a stark warning against management failing to effectively solve problems and allowing the wrong things to happen.

Admittedly, solving problems is not easy. If it were, there would be far fewer management failures to point to. The inherent underlying challenges in effective problem solving are first recognizing when problems occur and then identifying what they are.

This difficulty in recognizing and identifying problems is likened to a primordial swamp. Beneath a swamp's murky waters lie hidden obstacles and dangers. It is a haven for parasites and predators who exploit being unseen and unhindered.

Those who are intent on quickly and safely passing through the swamp find themselves at its mercy. They trip and fall and are delayed and injured while trying to negotiate its hidden obstacles. Progress in such an environment is uncertain and costly, but it can be remedied by one act: draining the swamp.

Once drained, the swamp loses its dehabilitating power. The obstacles and dangers are no longer hidden. Those passing through can clearly identify the obstacles and then effectively address them.

A swamp serves as a fitting metaphor for the difficulties management faces in solving problems. In order to solve problems, management must first recognize and identify them. To do this, management must drain the swamp.

This problem-solving capability is acquired through practicing the learned disciplines of management. For example input is obtained through measuring performance, gauging how well activities are performed and through following up on how well the executed activities have been performed, assessing whether ideal performance has been obtained. If it has not been achieved, management is alerted to a problem's existence, thus providing a ready-made context to identify what the problem was. Once identified, management is in position to take the appropriate action to solve the problem.

This carefully choreographed problem recognition and identification process has been documented through real-time reporting. As real-time performance information is disseminated throughout the organization, it enhances management's collective problem-solving capability by making unsolved problems everyone's problems.

Therefore, the systematic practice of the learned disciplines of management drains the swamp. It gives management the capability to solve problems, enabling management to make the right things happen. After all, solving problems is what effective management does, enhancing their effectiveness and ensuring their success. Effective problem solving incorporates five essential practices:

1. Recognize, identify, and understand the problem.

2. Determine if the problem is worth solving.

3. Determine which problem solution to implement.

4. Take action to solve the problem.

5. Monitor if the problem has been solved.

## Recognize, Identify, and Understand the Problem

The first problem-solving practice is to recognize, identify, and understand the problem. Many problems are unknown or not fully understood. Socrates, the Greek philosopher, rightly said twenty-four centuries ago, "We shall be better, braver, and more active men if we believe it right to look for what we do not know."[2]

To be effective problem solvers, management must fully grasp what they do not know. They must actively pursue the problem's presence, nature, and solution. Obtaining this knowledge is crucial. Problems waste valuable resources and produce unwanted results, thus undermining an organization's effectiveness and efficiency. Therefore, management must become problem experts, recognizing when and where problems occur, identifying what they are, and understanding how and why they happen so that they can be mitigated or eliminated.

Discovering problems is a thrilling process. Until they are discovered, these unknown problems unhinge performance and undermine success. Once the problems are recognized, management then has the opportunity to address the problems so that the expected performance outcomes can be obtained.

This is an essential first step, for only until management recognizes, identifies, and understands the problem can they take the appropriate action to solve it. As George Washington often liked to say, "Errors once discovered are more than half amended."[3]

Let me share an example that illustrates management's need to recognize, identify, and understand problems. The CEO of a business to business company hired my firm to deploy the learned disciplines of management. However, the company's managers believed they were already doing an excellent job. Consequently, they resented the hiring of an outside consultant to help them manage more effectively.

Their seeming success contributed to their self-assurance. For example, the company was a leader in its field. Over the past five years, it had maintained double-digit sales growth and was profitable (comparable to the middle-tier companies in its industry).

Because of this success, the company's managers strongly opposed the CEO's decision to retain my firm. They saw the CEO's decision as a meddlesome intrusion that wasted their time and the company's money. The only defense the CEO offered was a "gut feeling" that hiring me was the right course. The CEO's intuition proved prescient.

Despite management's opposition, the consulting project went forward. After several weeks, the seven learned disciplines were developed, designed, and deployed in the company's four largest departments. It was then that management began receiving real-time performance information that stripped away their smug self-satisfaction. The four departments had reported 937 documented problems during the first week.

These 937 problems represented a far different reality than management had assumed or recognized, thus contributing to their shock and dismay. They were problems that had been occurring day in and day out, hidden and misunderstood. Some documented problems had been occurring for several days, some for weeks, while still others had been occurring for months and some for years.

The first department's measured weekly performance was 33 percent. Its 67 percentage points performance shortfall was explained by 310 documented problems.

The second department's measured weekly performance was 42 percent. Its 58 percentage points performance shortfall was explained by 135 documented problems.

The third department's measured weekly performance was 35 percent. Its 65 percentage points performance shortfall was explained by 215 documented problems.

Finally, the fourth department's measured weekly performance was 38 percent. Its 62 percentage points performance shortfall was explained by 277 documented problems.

With 937 unrecognized but now documented problems, you may conclude that this management team was particularly inept for having allowed so many problems to occur for so long. But as we will see, that was not the case. What is true is that they lacked the management disciplines to recognize, identify, and understand problems. The surfacing of unrecognized problems is typical where, as was the case here, the learned disciplines of management were not practiced and the wrong things were allowed to happen.

The ability to recognize and identify problems was management's first acquired capability in solving problems. Although this was an important first step in solving problems, it was not the end but the end of the beginning. Soon, the managers were using this information to understand the nature of the problems so that they could develop solutions to solve them.

Evidence that management now had the tools to solve problems was not the 937 reported problems during the first week but the number of problems reported ten weeks later, which totaled only 66. Along with solving so many problems came a dramatic improvement in performance. Resources were used more effectively and efficiently, causing the four departments' collective measured performance to rise from 37 percent to over 70 percent. Improved profitability was another benefit gained from management's problem-solving capability. Profitability had improved 4 percentage points (representing millions of dollars). The company's enhanced profit performance placed it in the top 10 percent of comparable companies, a significant improvement over its mid-tier standing only a year before.

It took the company's managers only ten weeks to demonstrate their ability to solve problems and make the right things happen. With the right management tools, they were able to recognize when problems happened, identify what the problems were, and understand how and why they arose. These problem-solving capabilities combined to enable management to arrive at and implement the appropriate problem-solving solution.

Understanding a problem can prove challenging. This is because problems can arise from many different sources. Some can come from external sources such as customers and suppliers. Others can come from internal sources such as employees or work practices. There are problems that can cascade from other problems, and there are problems that can stem from other problems thrice removed. Additionally, unintended problems can result from well-meaning but unknowing managers who try to fix problems they don't fully understand.

Before managers can effectively solve problems, they first must thoroughly understand them. Recall in chapter 2 how Toyota executive Taiichi Ohno enjoined management to ask "why" five times in organizing an activity. He implored management to use the same rigorous approach in understanding problems. Here, he gives the following example:

> When confronted with a problem, have you ever stopped and asked why five times? It is difficult to do so even though

it sounds easy. For example, suppose a machine stopped functioning:

1. "Why did the robot stop?" The circuit has overloaded, causing a fuse to blow.
2. "Why is the circuit overloaded?" There was insufficient lubrication on the bearings, so they locked up.
3. "Why was there insufficient lubrication on the bearings?" The oil pump on the robot is not circulating sufficient oil.
4. "Why is the pump not circulating sufficient oil?" The pump intake is clogged with metal shavings.
5. "Why is the intake clogged with metal shavings?" Because there is no filter on the pump.[4]

Although this is an example drawn from heavy industry, it is nevertheless a helpful practice when dealing with all kinds of problems in all kinds of industries. Continually asking why a problem occurred results in a manager obtaining a deeper understanding of the problem. Once this is obtained, management is ready to determine if the problem is worth solving.

## Determine If the Problem Is Worth Solving

The second problem-solving practice may seem counterintuitive. But not all problems are worth solving. This may sound strange, but ironically, there are solutions to problems that cost more than the problem itself. There are solutions that are more troublesome than the problem itself. Thoroughly understanding the problem enables management to answer the question, is the problem worth solving? That is, are the problem's cost and consequences compelling enough for management to try to find a solution to the problem?

To answer this question, management must deeply understand the problem. A cost-benefit analysis is undertaken to answer the following questions: What does the problem cost? What benefit is there in solving the problem? Do the solution's benefits compellingly outweigh the problem's cost? If not, the problem is left alone.

Finding a compelling solution to the problem is imperative. It must be demonstrated that a solution is worthwhile. This requires that the solution's benefits be framed and contextualized. It must be clear that taking action to solve the problem outweighs not doing so. Many times, problems continue because management has not made a persuasive case to solve the problem.

For example, while consulting a large commercial products company, I observed the adversarial relationship between its Sales and Accounting Departments. Over time, the two departments had settled into an intractable state where they simply complained about the other department's performance rather than offer constructive solutions to the problems. For instance, accounting personnel complained salespeople had not given them the information they needed to effectively do their job. Salespeople complained that accounting imposed bureaucratic paperwork and policies on them that hindered their sales efforts. Unfortunately, the constant bickering did nothing to constructively address the problems, which continued because management had failed to find compelling solutions to them.

The stalemate between the two departments continued until management was able to frame the problem in a compelling way. This happened as the accounting manager, using real-time reported performance information, extrapolated the various problems' cost (and indirectly the benefits). He was able to show that his employees were averaging 35 hours per week trying to resolve problems caused by the sales department. These problems had a tangible cost: $45,000 per year in wasted accounting wages.

The accounting manager shared this information with the

sales manager. When the sales manager saw the problems' cost, he agreed something had to be done to solve it. Documenting the problems' cost made a compelling argument, breaking the long-standing impasse between the departments. The following week, the sales manager issued new sales policies and procedures to his salespeople. These policies and procedures required the salespeople to submit timely, complete, and accurate information to the Accounting Department.

The sales manager believed this action had solved the problem—that is, until the following week when the Accounting Department documented further salespeople-related problems. Although the number of sales-related problems had dramatically declined, there were still problems enough, representing $24,000 in wasted annual accounting wages. It turned out there were several recalcitrant salespeople ignoring the new policies.

The names of these salespeople, the problems they caused, and the cost to address them had been documented and reported and passed on to the sales manager. No longer was accounting perceived as "a bunch of whiners and complainers." Instead, the sales manager was given specific, creditable, real-time performance information to identify the problems.

With this information, the sales manager took action to address these problems. He met with each salesperson listed on the report, sharing the problems each had caused and what they cost the company. Using this feedback, the sales manager underscored the salespeople's need to adhere to the new policies. If they continued to ignore the new policies, accounting personnel would again document it. And when this happened, they would be back in his office discussing the issue once more.

This reporting of real-time performance information proved effective in addressing the problems caused by the Sales Department. Even though the Accounting Department continued to document problems, for the first time in years salespeople were not the source.

As this example illustrates, making a compelling argument—

framing why a problem is worth solving—prompts management action. The sharing of a problem's cost reinforces the need to quickly find and implement a solution to the problem.

## Determine Which Problem Solution to Implement

The third problem-solving practice, once it is determined the problem is worth solving, is to arrive at solutions worth implementing. Often, more than one solution is found. As a result, these various solutions are analyzed to determine which solution best solves the problem. Each solution's costs and benefits are scrutinized to decide which solution most compellingly solves the problem, thus triggering management action to implement it.

For example, a heart pacemaker manufacturer hired my firm. The company's management was struggling to produce enough pacemakers to meet the medical community's growing demand. This struggle was especially evident in the plant's Final Assembly Department, whose inadequate output prevented patients from getting the devices they so desperately needed.

I quickly immersed myself in the Final Assembly Department's operations. My first priority was to recognize, identify, and understand the department's problems and to come up with as many viable solutions to them as possible. With this focus, I quickly encountered a significant problem.

The Final Assembly Department had a substantial production bottleneck. Altogether, the department performed about a dozen core assembly processes. All the processes, save one, had the capacity to produce at least six hundred units. The one process that did not was the industrial x-ray station. Its production capacity was only five hundred units.

Finding a manufacturing bottleneck surprised management. They believed the plant's monthly manufacturing capacity was six hundred devices, not five hundred. This assumption overlooked or did not properly take into account the x-ray station's limited capacity. Consequently, the company's salespeople, who worked closely with cardiac surgeons, were selling six hundred heart pacemakers per month while the plant was actually manufacturing only five hundred pacemakers. This shortfall of one hundred devices was causing havoc.

Having identified the problem, I had to answer the question, was the problem worth solving? This required framing and contextualizing the problem's cost. My analysis showed that the final assembly bottleneck was costing the company over $2.4 million in lost revenue per year. Furthermore, there was a waiting list of sick patients in desperate need of the company's heart pacemakers. These factors made the problem worth solving if a compelling solution could be found.

With a problem worth solving, I set about trying to find a compelling solution worth implementing. The most obvious solution was to outsource x-raying the units. However, company management immediately ruled this option out, since x-raying the pacemakers' internal components (to ensure they were properly in place inside their sealed case) was a crucial quality-control process that was not trusted to an outside contractor.

The next solution I evaluated was to acquire another x-ray system. The department had enough adjoining space to accommodate a second x-ray station. However, the costs to purchase, install, and forgo production while a second station was set up was over $4 million. Although this amount would be recouped within two years, I continued to look for another more compelling problem solution—one that would not be summarily dismissed or cost so much.

I settled on trying to find ways to increase the x-ray station's current capacity. I concentrated on this third option, spending the next several days observing how the x-ray station functioned, asking the x-ray technicians "why" many times.

I observed the technician first placing four heart pacemakers on a metal tray. The tray was then placed into the x-ray machine where the devices were x-rayed. Afterward, the x-ray film was removed from the machine and developed. The developed film was then placed on a light board where the technician studied the images to make sure that all the components were in their proper place inside the unit's case. Once approved, the units were then passed on to the next final assembly process.

The x-ray station was operating twenty-four hours a day, seven days a week. When an x-ray technician took a break, another team member filled in. I also discovered the x-ray system being used was the fastest, highest-capacity system available on the market.

So far, my endless questions and constant observations did not produce any glaring operating deficiencies. As time passed, I began to question whether I would be able to find another more compelling solution to the problem. That was until the day I watched the technician study the developed x-ray film on the light board. I noticed that the pacemaker's outer case took up much of the film's image area. This was unnecessary, since the outer case had no internal components to be x-rayed.

I asked the technician if we could try an experiment. It seemed to me that five units could be arranged on the metal tray (instead of the usual four) if parts of the outer cases were excluded from the image. Since x-raying the outer cases was unnecessary, I thought this might be the breakthrough I was looking for.

The technician replied, "Hmm...we have never done that before. I am not comfortable trying a new, unapproved x-ray method."

"Let's treat this x-ray simply as an experiment," I said." You should of course x-ray the units as you normally would. But I'd like to have an x-ray of five units on the metal tray to see if it shows each unit's internal components. If it doesn't work, all we have done is waste one x-ray image. But if it does work, we may have found a solution to our problem."

"Okay. On that basis, I'll give it a try." He then he carefully placed five units on the metal tray and x-rayed them.

Soon afterward, we had the developed x-ray film on the light board. As the technician scanned the film's images, he excitedly exclaimed, "This could work!" Sure enough, there on the film, clearly in the field of view, were all five units' internal components that required inspection.

The next day I submitted the "experimental" x-ray image to the company's quality engineers. They reviewed the image and approved Final Assembly's new method of x-raying five units at a time. Not only had I found a solution to the problem, but I also had found the most compelling solution to the problem.

This solution was compelling because it had no additional cost. In fact, there was immediate savings as x-ray processing expense was reduced 25 percent. More important, however, was the immediate increase in production. Using the new x-ray method (x-raying five units at a time instead of four) resulted in an immediate jump in the x-ray station's capacity to 625 units. No longer was the x-ray station a production bottleneck. As a result, the plant was able to manufacture six hundred pacemaker units, allowing it to meet monthly sales demand. Waiting patients would receive their heart pacemakers, and the company's revenues would increase $2.4 million. I had found a compelling solution to a problem worth solving. The solution was so compelling that it was acted on that very day.

## Take Action to Solve the Problem

The previous example brings us to the fourth problem-solving practice: taking action to solve the problem. As the example above illustrated, recognizing, identifying, and understanding a problem leads to determining if the problem is worth solving. If it is, it leads to trying to find a compelling solution to the problem. When a compelling solution has been found, it prompts management to take action to solve the problem.

Taking effectual action has six salient phases: it specifically identifies what actions are to be taken, it measures the actions, the actions are translated into executable steps, the steps are assigned to be implemented, those assigned have a specific deadline to complete them, and the deadlines are followed up on to confirm they are completed when due.

Taking action is problem solving's climax. All the other problem-solving practices support this fourth practice. For taking action leads to solving the problem, enabling management to make the right things happen.

Therefore, it is incumbent on management to act swiftly and decisively to implement problem solutions. This is what effective management does. This is what a powerful, self-reinforcing management culture promotes. This action-taking expectation is reinforced during each employee follow-up session. It is reinforced during each daily management meeting. And it is reinforced during each weekly executive management meeting.

In these meetings, the problems are recognized, identified, and understood. The problems' costs and benefits are determined, and when appropriate, problem solutions are sought, framed, and put into context. The seeming best solutions are chosen, and management acts to implement them, anticipating the problems will be solved.

### Monitor If the Problem Has Been Solved

The fifth and final problem-solving practice is to monitor if the problem has been solved. Yes, a seemingly compelling solution has been chosen and implemented. But did it work? To confirm that it has, problem solving requires monitoring the situation. The reported real-time performance information is evaluated to confirm whether the problem has in fact been solved. Real-time reporting also provides feedback to determine if the solution may have caused other problems.

Monitoring problem-solving solutions is necessary to ensure that the right action was taken. Sometimes there are unintended consequences. Sometimes the solution unexpectantly costs more than anticipated. Sometimes the "solution" does not work. Through constant monitoring, these possible outcomes are recognized and acted on.

The process of choosing a solution, implementing it, and measuring whether it achieves the expected performance outcomes is an endless cycle. Real-time reporting gives management performance information to monitor performance results until the problem is solved. Afterward, real-time performance information continues to be disseminated to ensure the problem-solving solutions endure, producing the expected performance results.

The ability to assess the implemented solution's efficacy through reported real-time feedback gives management confidence to act decisively. If management discovers the implemented solution did not work as intended, no matter. Immediate action can now be taken to remedy the situation. The solution can be modified or replaced, and the change monitored until a successful outcome is achieved.

Management rigorously practicing problem solving has many benefits. When the wrong things happen, they are quickly identified and addressed. This focus on making the right things happen enhances performance outcomes and fosters a culture where performance continually improves. Improving performance maximizes resources and results, causing them to be used more efficiently and effectively. This translates into increased productivity and profitability, enhanced competitiveness, and an organizational culture where aims are met and employees thrive.

These are appealing benefits, but they are not always easily obtained. Problem solving is difficult and challenging. Problem solving heightens conflict as individuals are forced to work together to solve problems. In organizations where conflict avoidance has been the norm, this is an unpleasant by-product.

Problem solving is demanding in other ways. It has been well said, half in jest, half in truth, that the largest room in the world is the room for improvement. So it is. Problem solving is a relentless process. Its rewards are balanced by its demands. It is management's job to strike a balance between these in order to obtain the benefits that befall the diligent and persevering.

## Conclusion

Problem solving is the learned disciplines of management's apex. Its practice complements and completes them. It complements them by eliminating the wrong things from happening. It completes them by making the right things happen. As it does so, it fulfills management's aims and ensures their success.

In the final chapter, we will take the seven learned disciplines of management to work. I will demonstrate how they are practiced both individually and collectively to form a coherent management system that effectively transforms a company's management team that is struggling to make the right things happen.

## Chapter 8

# Deploying the Disciplines

You're broke.
—Jim Burkett

The preceding chapters have shown how each of the seven learned disciplines of management is practiced. In this chapter, I'll show how the seven disciplines are practiced systematically — that is, individually, interdependently, and collectively. This final chapter also serves as the book's conclusion, where each management discipline is developed, designed, deployed, and practiced to form a comprehensive management system that enables management to make the right things happen.

To do this, I will take you along with me on an actual consulting engagement, where I have been hired to implement the learned disciplines of management. I'll recount, step-by-step, how this is done. Along the way, you will meet a struggling management team that has allowed the wrong things to happen. These wrong things have made carrying out the company's essential activities problematic.

The consulting project provides a familiar backdrop, demonstrating how a beleaguered management team's effectiveness is enhanced and its success secured through practicing the learned disciplines of management. These disciplines allow management to accomplish more with them than they ever could have done without them.

It was a Saturday morning, just after breakfast, when my office phone rang. A businessman was on the line, whom we'll call Andrew. After a brief introduction, Andrew asked if my consulting firm might be able to help his company.

Calls like this one always come as a surprise. After consulting management over a thirty-five year period, you'd think I would have grown accustomed to them. But in fact I am always taken aback when someone turns to me for help. These calls are also exciting. For it is very rewarding to empower people to make the right things happen.

I asked Andrew about his business and his concerns so that I could determine if my firm could be of help. Andrew began with his company's history. Several years ago, Andrew and his business partner, whom we will call Peter, started Rebuild It (not the company's actual name but a fabricated name). Rebuild It specialized in restoring storm-damaged homes. Over the years, the construction company had experienced dramatic sales growth while producing solid profits.

But as the company's sales grew, so did the number of employees, contractors, and customers. The activities that sustained the company's success also grew in volume, variety, and complexity. These factors were now overwhelming management's ability to effectively manage the activities.

The result? Wrong things were happening more and more frequently. Andrew termed these developments "unwanted drama." Apparently, Rebuild It's management did not have the ability to prevent them. Obtaining the right outcomes was getting increasingly difficult and costing additional resources, which eroded profits and created a cash shortage despite the company's growing sales.

Andrew expressed a sinking feeling that his company was going in the wrong direction, as Rebuild It's management was constantly reacting to problems. However, Andrew and Peter were stymied as to what to do about it. Peter thought restructuring Rebuild It's various departments was the answer.

He believed a more decentralized organizational structure would give management greater control.

Andrew wasn't sure restructuring was the answer to the problems. He did not think restructuring got to the root of the continuing drama. Somehow his management team needed to control how employees performed their assigned activities. If his management team could not do this, he was sure the problems would persist regardless of how the organization was structured. The question for Andrew was how to do this.

Andrew also wondered out loud if the company's current problems were because one or more of his managers were not capable of effectively managing. If this was the case, he wanted a way to assess their capability so that inept managers could be replaced.

Andrew and Peter were unable to agree on a plan to address the company's growing performance issues. Andrew suggested that it was time to get some outside advice, and Peter agreed. It was that conversation that prompted his phone call to me.

I asked Andrew about his and Peter's backgrounds, including their experience and education. Andrew replied that he had an MBA and twenty years' experience in management, finance, and information technology. This included several years with a national managing consulting firm. Peter had twenty-five years' sales and sales management experience with a half-dozen companies.

I asked Andrew what were his and Peter's responsibilities at Rebuild It. Andrew said that he managed Rebuild It's operations, which included customer service, finance, information technology, project management, and procurement. There were about twenty people who performed these activities. Peter's responsibilities included overseeing marketing and sales. This also involved managing about twenty salespeople.

Over the course of our conversation, Andrew repeatedly

expressed his growing anxiety over how his company was being managed. He believed his business had crossed a threshold—an inexplicable tipping point where the company could quickly unravel and fail if it could not be managed more effectively.

I wondered how Rebuild It was being managed. Was the company's management practicing the fundamental management disciplines, or was their practice incomplete or nonexistent? I sought to answer this question by asking Andrew how his management team went about managing.

For example, I brought up measuring performance, stressing the underlying principle that you cannot manage what you don't measure. Andrew said performance measurement was not being done.

I introduced the discipline of executing, explaining how assigning, engaging, and empowering employees to perform essential activities made effective execution possible. Andrew replied that his managers had no formal executing method but that they assumed their employees knew what activities to do and tried their best to carry them out.

I explained management's need to practice following up to obtain actionable feedback, align activities to produce expected results, instill employee cooperation and accountability, and reinforce making the right things happen. Andrew said management followed up only when they had to—that is, when things went wrong.

I introduced real-time reporting, emphasizing the need to share real-time performance information throughout an organization. I stressed that real-time feedback was necessary so that management could assess performance and highlight problems to take the appropriate action. Andrew said his company used monthly accounting reports to help manage performance. He acknowledged that this approach wasn't too effective in addressing the underlying performance issues.

I emphasized the need to rigorously practicing problem solving to make the right things happen. Andrew conceded that this area was his management team's greatest weakness as his management team constantly reacted to problems instead of proactively solving them.

"Andrew, your answers to my questions are telling," I said. "It appears that you and your management team are not practicing the fundamental management disciplines. Without these, management is forced to manage by the seat of their pants, to use an old aviation term. That is, they are forced to rely on their instincts to manage. This approach makes for ineffective management and unsatisfactory results—an apprehensive mix for sure.

"To be effective, managers must avoid flying by the seat of their pants. This requires that they practice seven learned disciplines of management. I have already asked you about several of these disciplines, and it seems your management team is not practicing any of them. That is regrettable, because your managers' success depends on their practice.

"Andrew, you initially asked about how my consulting firm might be able to help your company. My firm's expertise is to facilitate management effectiveness through practicing the learned disciplines of management; enabling managers to make the right things happen.

"The process is a simple one. It involves tailoring each management discipline to fit your organization's needs and then deploying them throughout your company. As the disciplines are deployed, your managers are trained to use them to manage more effectively. A consulting project concludes when your management team is practicing the learned disciplines of management." I waited for Andrew's response.

"To be honest," Andrew said, "we have done a poor job giving our managers the tools they need to be effective. I believe we have hampered our employees by neglecting to identify and solve the problems they encounter. As a result, problems have bogged down our employees as they struggle to produce the right outcomes and our managers are stymied as they struggle to manage successfully. I'd like to explore further how we can give our managers and employees the tools they need to be successful. Let's schedule another meeting and ask Peter to join us."

I asked Andrew if Peter had the same perspective as he did.

"I don't think Peter does," Andrew said. "Growing sales is Peter's focus, and thanks to his ability, we don't have a sales problem. But despite Peter's focus, the daily drama that plays out around here is increasingly frustrating and distracting him. He sees the drama and the underlying problems that cause it as potentially holding us back from growing sales further. I think he will be willing to meet with you if you can offer us a practical way to manage more effectively. I'll ask him, and if he is not interested, I'll let you know, but otherwise, plan on meeting us. During the meeting, give us a formal consulting proposal that clearly demonstrates the benefits and details the cost, including how long it will take."

I told Andrew I'd prepare a consulting proposal and that I looked forward to meeting him and Peter to discuss it. I hung up the phone and reflected on the conversation. I was confident Rebuild It's management needed the learned disciplines of management to put an end to the unceasing drama. I was also hopeful that I could persuade Andrew and Peter to hire my consulting firm to develop and deploy them.

Preparing for the upcoming meeting, I researched Rebuild It's industry. I discovered that the top companies had averaged 6 percent profit on sales. I would compare this profit to Rebuild It's. Given what Andrew had told me, I was certain the company wasn't anywhere near this profit level. How could they be, given Rebuild It's managers were not practicing the fundamental management disciplines?

Assuming Rebuild It's profitability was less than 6 percent, I would use this result to contrast and quantify ineffective management's cost. I would argue that giving management a comprehensive system for managing would enhance management effectiveness and enable the company to produce a 6 percent profit. I'd point out that improved management effectiveness would not only pay for my consulting fees but also sustain sales growth, inculcate excellent performance, and establish healthy profits. I was counting on a large gap that would give me greater leverage in persuading Andrew and Peter to go forward with the consulting project.

It was an overcast and frigid winter morning when I drove up to Rebuild It's headquarters, which was situated in a modern, wood-clad cluster of office suites. I parked my car and briskly walked to the entrance.

At the door, a receptionist greeted me and quickly led me to an office where Andrew was waiting. Peter soon joined us and abruptly got the meeting underway by asking, "What do you have for us?"

I began my presentation: "My firm's aim is to give your management team the tools they need to manage more effectively and consists of seven learned disciplines of management. During a consulting engagement, these disciplines are custom-tailored and then deployed so that your management team can better manage essential activities. When these activities are effectively managed, they maximize results and resources, thus reducing expenses and increasing profits."

"What are the seven disciplines?" Peter asked.

"Planning, organizing, measuring performance, executing, following up, real-time reporting, and problem solving," I said.

I gave Peter and Andrew several examples how practicing the

learned disciplines of management had enabled management to maximize resources and results. I also shared with them several instances how the learned disciplines of management might be applied to Rebuild It's operations.

Coming to what I hoped would be my most persuasive argument, I stated, "My research indicates that the top companies in your industry average 6 percent profitability. Given the right tools, your management team has the potential to achieve this profit level as well."

It was at this point that I lost control of the meeting. My imagined compelling argument unraveled as Peter abruptly interrupted me, emphatically stating, "Our company is doing better than 6 percent. I don't know what companies you are referring to as being best, but they don't compare to our profitability." Reaching for his calculator, Peter entered from memory several sets of numbers. Looking up, he pronounced, "This past year, Rebuild It's profitability was 13 percent. We are much more profitable than the companies you cite. Why would we consider hiring you? So we can make a lousy 6 percent?"

Peter's pronouncement stunned me. The thought that his company was making a 13 percent profit (double the industry's best financial results) seemed inconceivable. An awkward silence settled over our meeting. Both Peter and Andrew were looking at me for a response, but I was left dumbfounded and speechless.

Finally, I answered, "Well...given your profit results...you're right. I can't see how I could be of much help."

Peter nodded in agreement, then Andrew spoke up. "We don't know what our company's profitability is. Our accounting firm is still working on last year's financials, and we don't expect they will be completed for another several weeks." Then turning to Peter, he asked, "How did you get your 13 percent profit number?"

"It's simple," Peter replied. "Our company has $1.2 million in accounts receivables. Since sales last year were $8.7 million, that means our company had a net profit of over 13 percent."

"I think your accounts receivable number is overstated," Andrew said. "I don't know the actual receivables total, but it is not anywhere close to being that high. I know Final Billing is trying to collect about $200,000. So if it is not in collections, it has not been billed and therefore it is not a receivable."

"Just last week each department gave us their work-in-progress dollar total," Peter said. "As I recall, Production had $700,000 and Final Billing had another $500,000 work in progress. This represents money that is owed to us, which, to my way of thinking, is profit."

"If the company is so profitable, why have we exhausted our bank credit line?" Andrew retorted. "Why can't we pay our bills? For example, why are we several months' past due on our largest invoices? And why are we struggling to come up with enough cash just to meet our payroll?"

"Our cash crunch is a simple timing issue," Peter quickly replied. "Although Rebuild It is an extremely profitable business, it is also a very seasonal one. At the moment, we are experiencing our lowest cash inflow. It always happens during this time of year when our sales are low and our expenses are at their highest. When the weather breaks in a couple of months, we will be able to start working again and the cash shortage will soon right itself. Besides, I think we can grow sales by another 35 percent this year. If so, the additional sales will easily cover any cash flow problems we have. Meanwhile, we just have to wait out this seasonal lull."

I spoke up. "Listening to you, it is obvious to me you don't really know what is happening in your business. So far I've heard a lot of guesswork, assumptions, and conjectures. Here you are, two months after the year has ended, and you still don't know how your business performed. You think you know. You are hoping you do. But based on the conversation I just heard, you don't actually know. Nor can you expect to. You and your management team don't have the tools to manage effectively.

"For example, you don't have timely feedback indicating how your business is performing. Instead, you are relying on accounting information to manage your business. This is a problem because accounting information was never intended to be used to manage day-to-day operations. It takes real-time performance information to do that.

"Andrew, you mentioned that you are waiting on last year's accounting results. Presumably this information will help you manage the company's essential activities. Indeed, these activities must be managed for the company to be successful. But here you are waiting for information to manage your business. Waiting is not managing. Consequently, your management team is not making the right things happen, but instead is allowing the wrong things to happen—the drama you referred to. To be effective, your managers need timely and reliable performance information.

"Having real-time performance information is one of the benefits of the learned disciplines of management. Without these tools, you are managing by the seat of your pants. This is a risky proposition because you don't have the necessary feedback to take the appropriate action."

"You're right," Andrew replied. "It's frustrating sitting here waiting for information we need to manage the business. It feels like we are in the dark about how the business is functioning. To your point, having timely performance information would certainly shine light on how our business is performing, giving our managers more control over operations."

"Although I know our company is very profitable, it does not mean it will stay that way," Peter said. "It seems to be getting harder and harder around here to get things done and done right. There is way too much drama. This isn't good for our customers, employees, or contractors, and it isn't good for our business. Perhaps our managers do need better tools to manage. If they had them, it could make a huge difference."

"That is the point, Peter," Andrew said. "We have not given our managers the tools they need. Yet we expect them to get the results as if they did have them. Meanwhile, how are we ever going to get control over the business unless we invest in these tools?

"The growth of our business has been phenomenal, but it feels like we are trying to hang onto a rocket ship. As we have hung on, the business fundamentals have been neglected—fundamentals like efficiently organizing our activities or giving our managers the information they need to manage effectively. Unless we take the time and money to make these fundamental changes, I don't see us getting any better. In fact, I see us getting a lot worse.

"I believe the consulting program Jim is proposing will give our managers the tools they need to effectively manage our business."

Peter looked at Andrew and said, "I don't have these tools in my tool kit, do you?"

"No, I don't, and we need these tools now!"

Peter turned to me and asked how long a consulting project would take, what it would cost, and the financial and operational improvements that could be expected.

I had anticipated these questions and laid out for Andrew and Peter what a Rebuild It consulting project entailed, including the project's scope, cost, duration, expected operational improvements, and the typical return on investment.

Peter and Andrew agreed to move forward with the project. We then set a date for the consulting engagement to begin. At the time, we had no idea that the learned disciplines of management would not only transform management effectiveness but also save the company from bankruptcy.

Several weeks later, on a bright, warm, spring morning, I arrived back at it Rebuild It's headquarters. I was ready to begin developing, designing, and deploying the learned disciplines of management.

Obviously the company's aim was to make a profit. What was still unknown was how much. The accounting firm had yet to complete the previous year's financials. They were still working on them and needed a few more weeks to finish them.

I was anxious to know the company's profitability. More importantly, the profit aim, whatever it was, had to be incorporated into the company's plan.

Rebuild It's management team had no such plan. Because of this, planning would be the first discipline to be deployed. Practicing the planning discipline would determine Rebuild It's overarching organizational aims (as well as each department's aims) and the means to obtain them.

I developed the plan beginning with the two aims that had already been stated: to obtain 13 percent profitability and to increase sales 35 percent.

Although Peter had pegged the company's profit at 13 percent, this had yet to be confirmed. Like Andrew, I was skeptical the profit level was this high. If it were, it made Rebuild It's business model an outlier where the fundamental management disciplines did not need to be practiced to achieve excellent results. From my experience, this was very unlikely.

An outlier or not, I knew once the planning discipline was deployed the company's profitability and many other questions would be answered. I needed to quickly develop the company's plan, and I would not wait for last year's financial accounting results to do so.

Rebuild It's plan took shape, fueled by real-time information. It would be information management could act on, not wait on. This entailed the plan having information that not only projected future performance but also provided timely updates as to how the company was actually performing against its plan. When actual performance was regularly compared to planned performance, it would give management actionable feedback to take the appropriate action.

The plan was laid out on a spreadsheet. The spreadsheet had fifty-two columns, and each column represented a week. For each week, the company's seasonally adjusted sales were calculated. The sales volume for the year could be adjusted to any given sales level with one spreadsheet input. In keeping with management's aim, this input was initially set for sales to increase 35 percent.

The projected weekly cash receipts were calculated from each week's projected sales. This calculation was based on how long, on average, it took customers to pay their invoices.

From the projected weekly cash receipts, the spreadsheet subtracted the projected cash expenses. This included both fixed (rent, payroll, etc.) and variable (material costs, commissions, etc.) expenses. These were entered in the week they were due. The resulting calculations projected Rebuild It's planned weekly cash on hand.

The plan also included weekly performance information that tracked the means for achieving the plan's aims (at this early stage in the consulting project, this information was in limited supply and would remain so until all the learned disciplines were deployed). For example, the plan included the number of planned and actually completed sales calls, the number of planned and actually completed construction projects, and each department's planned and actual measured performance.

The plan would be updated each week with actual data

so that the plan had both actual results and projected results (a bold vertical line indicated actual data to its left, projected information to its right). When a week concluded, another week would be added to the spreadsheet, projecting the plan out fifty-two weeks.

When complete, the plan (postulated on the spreadsheet) gave management information projecting how the company would perform week-by-week and cumulative for the year. As the plan was updated each week, it gave management actual data. Thus, when the actual weekly results were compared to the planned weekly results, it gave management feedback as to how the company was performing against the plan.

Setting up Rebuild It's plan in this fashion allowed me to deduce the company's planned profit performance for the remainder of the year. If I wanted to approximate profit using accounting methods, all I would have to do was add or subtract any noncash adjustments to projected cash flow—adjustments such as depreciation, amortization, and accrual charges (which in Rebuild It's case were minimal).

I was anticipating seeing the plan's results. When all the data was entered and the calculations were made, the plan would depict the company's planned profit for each week and cumulatively for the year. The completed plan would put an end to speculating what the company's profitability might be and going forward avert having to guess at it.

It took two days to complete Rebuild It's plan. When it was finished, I quickly scanned the results. At first I thought I had made a mistake in putting the spreadsheet together. Each week's projected cash flow showed cash losses. These cash losses continued to mount as the year progressed, resulting in a very substantial cumulative loss.

Certain that I had made a mistake I combed the spreadsheet looking for data entry and formula calculation errors. But there were no errors—the spreadsheet was correct. Instead of a 13 percent profit, the company's plan projected a $400,000 cash loss (assuming a 35 percent increase in sales). If the company's sales did not grow but remained the same, the plan's projected cash loss was $700,000.

The plan's results stunned me. The plan showed not only that Peter's profit assumptions were incorrect but also that the company was insolvent and would go bankrupt if management did not act quickly to remedy the situation. The plan's results explained Andrew's growing anxiety and the company's inability to pay its bills. The plan showed the company was not anywhere close to making a 13 percent profit, and it also showed growing sales by 35 percent was unlikely. In fact, after twelve weeks, actual sales were down 20 percent over the previous year.

These dismal results left me pondering what the company's planned aims should be for the coming year. Although the top financially performing companies were achieving 6 percent profitability, Rebuild It's managers were obviously not presently in this group. Also, given the company's recent sales performance, it was not likely to increase sales by 35 percent. Therefore, it was imprudent to plan for a sizable sales increase. In any event, it would be incumbent on Andrew and Peter to come up with realistic planned aims.

One thing was clear: Rebuild It's management had a daunting challenge ahead. For example, just to break even (on static sales), the company's management team would have to reduce expenditures $700,000. To make a 6 percent profit, management would have to reduce expenditures another $500,000 (6 percent x $8,700,000) for a combined $1,200,000 reduction in annual expenditures. Only time would tell if the management team could achieve this expense reduction and resulting profit level. But before Rebuild It's management could achieve these benchmarks, they had to have the management tools to manage results and resources more effectively and efficiently. Giving them these tools was why I had been hired.

Planning, the first of these tools, was now deployed. Its practice exposed the company's unintended aims and ineffective means. Consequently, a new plan had to be developed—one that had the right aims and the necessary means to obtain them.

I was anxious to share the plan's findings with Andrew and Peter. I was curious how they would take the news. I was also intent on eliciting their input in crafting a new plan. How they navigated this next phase would prove insightful and expose whether they were they able to tackle the challenges ahead.

The next morning, the three of us gathered in Andrew's office. Using my laptop and an attached projector, I displayed Rebuild It's current plan (presented in a spreadsheet) onto the office wall. As I did so, I explained how the plan worked. Scrolling to the spreadsheet's last page, I showed the planned cumulative results and declared, "You're broke! Even if sales increase 35 percent, the plan shows you will lose $400,000. If sales remain at last year's level, which is more likely, given your recent sales history, you will lose $700,000. In either case, unless you act quickly or have an extra $1 million sitting around, your company is going bankrupt. It is already insolvent."

Peter looked dismissively at the plan's numbers and declared, "This is bogus! Your numbers are so out of touch with reality I won't even consider them. This is outrageous! Where did you get this information anyway?"

Before I could answer, Andrew spoke up. "Earlier this morning Jim asked me to look over the spreadsheet to confirm the plan's numbers and results. After reviewing the plan, I believe it accurately projects our company's cash flow. Peter, to answer your question, the information on the spreadsheet comes directly from our company records. This includes our weekly reports, banking statements, payroll reports, and monthly financials."

Peter was unconvinced. "I want to see that for myself. Hand me the records this spreadsheet claims to show," he said.

Andrew gathered a stack of papers and handed them to Peter. Peter looked through the papers and then back at me. "I am familiar with this information," he said. "Show me where it is on your spreadsheet."

Painstakingly, I authenticated the spreadsheet's data. I explained, amid Peter's numerous questions, how the information came together to depict each week's projected cash flow and how these projections were cumulated to show the referenced annual losses.

When I was done, Peter contritely acknowledged, "Well, I guess the company is not the cash cow I assumed it was."

Thereafter we discussed what the company's aims should be. Peter was confident, despite the recent results, that his sales team could at least maintain last year's sales volume. Additionally, both executives wanted to plan for the highest possible profit level. Accordingly, the company's planned profit aim was established at 6 percent.

From these new aims evolved the necessary means. Specifically, it caused us to develop three chief means to reduce cash expenditures by $1.2 million. The first means was to reduce discretionary spending in areas such as advertising, marketing, travel, meals, and entertainment. The second means was to find ways to reduce construction labor and material costs. The third means entailed managing more effectively and efficiently Rebuild It's results and resources, including its forty employees.

The new plan produced decisive action. In the coming days, Rebuild It's management team reduced discretionary spending and construction labor and material costs by $600,000. The company was halfway toward reducing cash expenditures by

$1.2 million and achieving its 6 percent profit aim.

The remaining $600,000 in expense reductions could only be achieved through more effective management, and this required that Rebuild It's management team practice the learned disciplines of management. But first these had to be deployed. For until management had the necessary tools to manage, there was little hope that $600,000 in additional expense reductions could be realized. This third means would inevitably make the difference between the company breaking even or making a profit.

Now it was up to me to develop, design, and deploy the learned disciplines of management in Rebuild It's four principal departments. I began with the Final Billing Department.

Final Billing had two primary tasks. The first was to determine how much money the company was owed when a construction project was completed (this amount being billed to the respective party for payment), and the second task was to collect the monies due (or past due) using traditional bill collection activities.

To carry out these two tasks, the department's employees had to perform a myriad of activities that had to be managed so that resources and results were maximized. To facilitate managing these activities required me to design or custom-tailor the learned disciplines of management to fit the department's particular needs. However, before I could begin designing the management disciplines, I first had to acquire a thorough understanding of all the activities the department performed.

To do this, I embedded myself in the department. I explained to the department's employees my purpose was to understand what they did and that this entailed my observing the activities they performed. I pointed out that as I watched them carry out activities, I would probably be asking a lot of questions—particularly as to why and how something was done. I explained that this approach (the practice of organizing) helped me to thoroughly understand what they did and allowed me to assess how efficiently and effectively the activities were carried out.

I settled into the department and began identifying the various activities. It was important to recognize each and every one, for they all had to be managed. Once the activities were identified, I carefully observed how they were performed.

As I observed each activity, its individual steps were broken down and documented. If I did not understand something, I asked "why" until I understood it. Inevitably, I asked a lot of questions to gain a practical understanding of each activity. When I finished observing an activity, believing I understood all its aspects, I would share this information with the department's employees and managers to confirm that I did in fact understand it.

Once I practically understood how an activity was carried out, I was then in a position to evaluate how well it was organized—that is, to assess whether it maximized resources and results. Ever mindful that this was the ultimate litmus test, I would continually ask if the activity was necessary, and if it was, was it being performed efficiently and effectively. If the answer was no, I would reorganize the activity to achieve this end.

Practicing organizing yielded many insights. The most disturbing was the large amount of cash that the department's various activities tied up. The department had approximately eighty backlogged job folders representing over $600,000. This was money the company was owed (an amount offset by expenses to determine profit) and, for a company struggling to pay its bills, represented a potential cash treasure trove—that is, if the activities could be better organized to free up the much-needed cash.

Of the eighty backlog job folders (representing forty business days to process), sixty had to have the final bill determined. Another twenty backlogged job folders were tied up in collections as Rebuild It's employees attempted to get these due and past due invoices paid.

As I observed the Final Billing activities being performed, two activities caught my attention. The first activity, processing insurance claims (representing 40 percent of the backlogged job folders), appeared to be ineffectively organized.

Processing an insurance claim involved faxing an invoice to the insurance company's claims payment center. Several days later, a Final Billing employee would phone the claim center's representative to try and confirm they received the invoice.

I saw that these insurance claim representatives were hard to reach. Often it required multiple phone calls and lot of wasted time to finally get an answer. When the answer did come, it was almost always the same: the fax had been received and the check was being processed and payment should be received within the next several business days.

This activity represented a lot of effort just to confirm a fax was received, especially when it was often confirmed that it had. I concluded the activity was not necessary and suggested an alternate solution be found.

Management agreed that the activity was redundant, which resulted in reorganizing the activity and eliminating follow-up phone calls altogether (unless the invoice was not paid within a set time period). This change allowed 40 percent of the job folders to flow more effectively through the department while using fewer resources (employees' time).

The second activity that caught my attention was preparing project invoices. This activity was performed inefficiently because of duplicated effort. Preparing an invoice took an average of eight minutes. However, I noted this activity was being done twice for each project (once for the insurance company's invoice and a second time for the customer's invoice). As a result, what should have been a one-time calculation taking eight minutes was instead taking sixteen minutes, causing Final Billing to take twice as long to prepare a job folder's invoices.

I asked an employee why both the insurance and customer invoices were not processed at the same time. I was told that it had never been done like that before—but it could be. She admitted there was no reason to do it twice.

As a result, management agreed to reorganize how invoices were processed. The newly organized activity had one person prepare both invoices, which cut processing time in half.

As these and other activities were reorganized, the Final Billing employees' effectiveness and efficiency was greatly enhanced. This was reflected in the number of backlogged job folders needing the final bill determined, which went from sixty job folders (representing $400,000) to three (representing $17,000). Much needed cash was now flowing quickly through the department into the company's coffers.

Practicing the organizing discipline laid the groundwork for measuring performance, another discipline to be deployed. Organizing had produced a list of all the activities the department performed. Now an ideal performance measure was derived for each activity on the list so that management could gauge how employees performed these activities. This was derived by frequently observing and measuring each of the activities being performed.

The performance measures were first used to establish how many employee hours were needed to complete the Final Billing Department's activities. Because the department was not performing ideally, I was forced to estimate what the department's performance could eventually be. Using this estimate, I calculated the number of employees the department would need (later, once all the disciplines were deployed, this estimate would be confirmed using actual real-time reported performance information).

The performance measures were also used to determine how much time an employee had available for additional activities. For example, measuring performance showed that each Final Billing employee had available two hours to perform collection activities. Based on this, each employee was assigned up to twenty-four collection calls per day (a collection call took five minutes, which, multiplied by twenty-four calls, equaled two hours).

Final Billing had twenty job folders totaling $200,000 in past-due invoices. However, in the past, the Final Billing employees rarely contacted these late-paying customers. For instance, one customer owed the company $13,000, an amount that was past due four months. Yet it had been nine weeks since a Final Billing employee called this customer to ask for prompt payment. In fact, the department's employees made only a handful of collection calls each day, meaning that only a small proportion of past due accounts were being contacted. Up until now, this performance went unnoticed, inadvertently allowing the wrong things to happen. Now, through practicing measuring performance, management had a means to gauge how well this activity was performed.

The executing discipline was deployed next. A checklist was developed for each employee, denoting what activities they were assigned to perform. The checklists were assembled on an electronic spreadsheet and printed out on paper for each employee to use. The spreadsheet was also used to record and calculate each employee's (and collectively each department's ) measured performance.

The department manager distributed the prepared checklists to the appropriate employees and explained that each listed activity was being assigned to the employee to perform.

Additionally, each activity now had an ideal performance measure the employee was expected to obtain (lacking any problems). The manager explained that the employee's performance would be periodically followed up on and measured and the performance results assessed and shared. If employees ran into a problem that prevented them from obtaining ideal performance, they were asked to document the problem and take the appropriate action to address it.

Executing now made management follow-up possible. This in turn generated actionable feedback that exposed the Final Billing Department's poor performance, including the many problems that plagued the department.

For example, during the first day, a Final Billing employee was assigned nineteen customers to contact whose invoices were past due. When management followed up on this employee, they discovered that the employee had contacted only seven customers due to several problems.

One problem was caused by the employee who believed her nineteen assigned calls were optional. Realizing this, the employee's manager took the opportunity to align the assigned activities with the expected results, correcting the employee's wrong assumptions and unsatisfactory performance. Another problem was the employee having to frequently restart her computer because of software glitches. Recognizing this problem for the first time, the manager took action and had the service provider update the software.

Following up had identified problems that management was able to quickly address; enabling management to reinforce making the right things happen. Now, late-paying customers were regularly being contacted, causing the number of past-due accounts to plummet.

Following up also enabled management to generate and gather real-time performance information. This collected performance information was shared throughout the organization through the practice of real-time reporting. Now, individual employees and managers alike received actual, accurate, and timely feedback to identify and solve problems.

Solving problems had long been neglected in this struggling company as the deployed disciplines soon revealed. However, as management began practicing the learned disciplines of management, first in Final Billing and later in the company's other departments, a constant stream of actionable feedback became available. The feedback was sobering.

For example, of the thirty-four employees whose performance was being measured, only one had measured performance above 40 percent (a Final Billing employee at 42 percent). The remaining employees had measured performance that ranged from 22 to 36 percent.

Countless documented problems explained the poor performance results. For example, twenty-one employees simply ignored performing their assigned activities (e.g., salespeople were assigned fifty sales calls to perform, but they completed, on average, only seven), two employees did not have enough work to do, and several employees spent their time correcting other employees' work before they could carry out their own work assignments.

When this and other feedback was reported to Andrew and Peter, they had markedly different reactions. Andrew clenched his jaw and retorted, "This will have to be addressed!" whereas Peter laughed out loud. However, despite their differing reactions, both Andrew and Peter became adept problem solvers.

For example, the system for managing showed that salespeople were not performing their assigned sales calls. This was clearly a problem, for the company's success depended on sales calls being made in order to generate sales. After investigating the problem, Andrew and Peter concluded the salespeople's compensation package was to blame.

The salespeople's compensation package paid a large base salary and a small commission (based on sales made). Since the company was essentially underwriting the salespeople's time, management assumed the salespeople would feel obligated to make their assigned sales calls. However, actionable feedback indicated this was not the case.

To solve the problem, Andrew and Peter redesigned the salespeople's compensation package. The new compensation package was a traditional incentive plan. It principally paid salespeople commissions based on performance (sales and sales calls performed). The new compensation package caused an upsurge in sales calls, which resulted in increased sales.

Practicing the learned disciplines of management transformed Rebuild It's management effectiveness. Consequently, as problems were identified and addressed, there was a lot less drama. Less drama translated into resources and results being maximized. Management's transformation was also reflected in Rebuild It's plan—expressly, in its markedly improved cash flow.

The company's management transformation was as dramatic as it was easy to measure. Before the learned disciplines were deployed, the company had a $700,000 (on static sales) planned cash loss. After practicing them, the company had a $900,000 planned cash surplus—a $1.6 million reversal.

This $1.6 million cash flow improvement reflected that management was now operating more effectively and efficiently, thus maximizing resources and results—the tangible results of making the right things happen.

Rebuild It's turnaround surprised Andrew and Peter. Although they were expecting a degree of improvement in how their company was managed and performed, they were caught off guard by the dramatic impact practicing the learned disciplines of management had on their management team.

Andrew and Peter were also pleased with the results. The company's unceasing drama had come to an end, as their management team became effective problem solvers. This translated into reduced costs and improved profitability; erasing a devastating cash deficit with a substantial cash surplus.

I too was pleased with the results. I had asserted that if management had the right tools, they could make the right things happen. An ensuing $1.6 million profit improvement made good on that assertion.

As for being surprised, I can't say that I was. My surprise in seeing the results of practicing the learned disciplines of management had come almost four decades ago in a Cell Subassembly Department. Since then, in all sorts of industries and departmental specializations, I have grown accustomed to seeing management transformed through their practice.

Just as the secret to Rebuild It's management's success was their skillful practice of the learned disciplines of management, so too does your success as a manager depend on skillfully practicing them.

It is my hope as we conclude this book that you too have discovered how to effectively practice the learned disciplines of management and will use them to make the right things happen.

# Appendix A

# Management: A Calling

To be at the head of a strong column of troops, in the execution of some task that requires brain, is the highest pleasure of war—a grim one and terrible, but which leaves on the mind and memory the strongest mark.

—William Tecumseh Sherman

During the sixteenth century, there arose a religious movement known as the Reformation. It was led by a group of Protestant reformers called Puritans (so named because they sought to purify the church). The Puritans relied on the Bible to direct their lives, and their application of God's word in relation to work still influences us today.

Prior to the Reformation, one's vocation (derived from vocare, a Latin verb meaning "to call") was narrowly seen as God calling individuals to specific roles in the church. For instance, it was believed that God called a man to serve as priest or missionary.

However, the Puritans rejected this limited vocational perspective. Instead, they saw God "calling" individuals not only to church roles but also to most secular occupations. Puritans believed God gave each person individual gifts, talents, aptitudes, and abilities that inevitably directed them toward their "chosen" occupation. Based on this perspective, the Puritans saw no distinction between a man called to be a church missionary and a man called to be a coal miner, a man called to be a church bishop and a man called to be a village blacksmith.

How about you? Are you called, irresistibly drawn to, the

management profession? Do you possess the talent, aptitude, and skill that confirm the calling? This is an important question and requires some reflection. Like many other professions, management is not for the indifferent and the unskilled—those not called.

A calling is confirmed when one's aspirations and aptitudes merge. Take, for instance, a person who desires to be a surgeon. Although this person may have a deep interest in the profession and a strong motivation to pursue it, these will count for little if this person lacks the necessary aptitudes (e.g., exceptional hand-eye coordination and finger dexterity) to be a surgeon.

In a similar vein, simply choosing (or being chosen) to be a manager is not the same as being called to the profession. Who says that just because you have an interest in managing and are prepared to work really hard at it that you'll be successful? Although interest and effort count for something, they alone are not enough. Without the requisite management skill, managerial success will be found wanting and work satisfaction elusive.

The relationship between skill and success is especially crucial in endeavors where management skill is essential for success. Although not all endeavors require a high degree of management skill, for those that do, it is essential that the management practitioner is skillful, that they possess a calling to the profession. For example, successfully launching an amphibious assault against an entrenched enemy requires a high degree of management skill. In such circumstances, it is obvious when the calling is present and painfully evident when it is not.

Unfortunately, many men and women become managers without first considering whether they are called to be a manager. Often, their unrelated skills recommend them for the job. For instance, they become management candidates because they are an accomplished technician, a successful salesperson, a resourceful engineer, or a gifted teacher. Unfortunately, success in these vocations does not automatically translate into having a management calling.

Prospective management candidates need to consider their calling, for there is a direct link between aptitude and success. This link cannot be assumed, for just as everyone is not born the same, so too not everyone possesses the same management aptitude to be successful.

Employers should also carefully consider whom they ask to become a manager. In their considerations, the prospective candidate's management aptitude should not be assumed but rigorously assessed. This is important, for although management skill can be enhanced, it cannot be acquired—despite many popular misconceptions. An employer's failure to accurately assess an employee's management aptitude is risky. It potentially places a person into a management position for which the person is destined to fail while at the same time depriving the organization of a valuable employee.

Take, for example, an exercise my mother participated in when she was employed at AT&T. At the time, she was an hourly employee being considered for a management position. Her manager had recommended her as a management candidate, and she was invited to take part in a weeklong management evaluation class (along with a dozen other aspirants). The class was designed to assess a candidate's management aptitude through various exercises and tests.

One such test was called the "Jigsaw Puzzle Task." The class was broken up into groups of four with one class member designated as the group leader. The group leader was asked to manage the group in assembling the jigsaw puzzle in the quickest time possible.

Gathering the group, the class evaluators would shout, "Go!" and then closely observe the designated group leader's actions while timing the exercise. The pressure to assemble the jigsaw puzzle as fast as possible caused the various group leaders to respond reflexively. As such, they inevitably took two common approaches—approaches the evaluators were anxious to observe.

The typical approach (keeping in mind these candidates were hourly employees used to doing the work themselves) was best described as a free-for-all. Although the group leader was charged with managing the group, this did not happen. Instead, the group leader's natural instinct was to try and get the puzzle assembled as quickly as possible, and how the leader did it gave the evaluators insight into the candidate's management aptitude. These candidates responded with a mad dash. They frantically started to sort the puzzle pieces themselves and quickly put them together while anxiously urging their teammates to do the same. Over the ruckus, the only occasional instructions heard from these team leaders was the call to "work faster, FASTER!" Not the apparent aptitude of a manager.

The second and much smaller candidate group took a significantly different and telling approach. These candidates' first action was not to start putting the puzzle pieces together themselves but to assign each team member a task. For instance, "Justin why don't you turn over the puzzle faces so we can see what we're looking for? Beth, please find all the straightedge border pieces and start putting them together. Bart, see that big red barn in the center of the picture? Why don't you find all the red pieces for it and put them together?"

It was only after all the team members were busily engaged would these team leaders touch their first puzzle piece. Throughout the exercise, they made sure each team member had a task to do before resuming putting the puzzle together themselves. Not only did this approach result in the shortest assembly times, but it also demonstrated to the observers those candidates who possessed management aptitude—the ability to work through others to effectively make the right things happen.

There are two positive outcomes for those who possess management aptitude: excellent results and deep satisfaction.

A case in point is William Tecumseh Sherman, one of the ablest field commanders in the American Civil War. Sherman reflects in his memoirs, "To be at the head of a strong column of troops, in the execution of some task that requires brain, is the highest pleasure of war—a grim one and terrible, but which leaves on the mind and memory the strongest mark."[1] Sherman's record in managing the battlefield produced exemplary results, and he passionately enjoyed his work—he had found his calling.

However, there are two common situations that cloud assessing a manager's calling. The first is where a manager's success is seen as confirmation of his calling. The second situation is where a manager's failure is seen as confirming their not being called to manage.

An example where a manager's success obscured her true management calling was the case of a manger we'll call Susan. Susan was a manager at a large industrial supply company I was hired to consult with that was struggling to make the right things happen. Despite growing sales, the company's profitability was declining. For every $100,000 sales increase, expenses increased commensurately, erasing any profits from the new sales. This inexplicable situation (where more sales produced fewer profits) had been occurring over the past several years. It also loomed into the future as the company was experiencing record sales but its projected profits were lower than the previous year.

The company's Customer Service Department was one department (among several others) that required more and more resources to get the job done. Susan, the department's manager, justified this expenditure by pointing out that her department bore the brunt of having to support the growing sales. But what Susan could not explain was why the Customer Service Department was using resources at a faster rate than sales were growing; this indicated that there were more issues involved than simply supporting additional sales growth.

In the past year, the department had hired several customer

service representatives. But despite this expenditure, Susan claimed she still did not have enough employees to complete all of the department's essential activities. Consequently, she had asked to hire more customer service representatives.

Susan had served as a customer service representative for eight years before being promoted to department manager (a job she had held for about a year). Over several weeks, I observed Susan and her department in action. Tellingly, no management disciplines were being practiced, explaining why it required more and more resources to complete the department's activities.

Meeting with the company's executives, I laid out my recommendations for the Customer Service Department. I shared the many problems I had observed, tracing the problems back to Susan not practicing the learned disciplines of management. I recommended that she be given the tools she needed to effectively manage her department. Executive management readily accepted my recommendations.

The following week, we deployed the learned disciplines of management in the Customer Service Department. For the first time, Susan had the tools to effectively manage. However, when the first week concluded, the department's initial results were disappointing. The department's measured performance was a paltry 22 percent. Susan was dismayed. She responded, "When I looked up from my desk, everyone seemed so busy."

To Susan's credit, she adapted to and seemingly embraced using the new management disciplines. In practicing them, she began to effectively manage her department. Over a period of several weeks, she identified and solved problems. This freed up resources that allowed the department to fulfill its growing work demands and caused Susan to cancel the request for additional new hires. Over a period of a few months, employees' measured performance jumped to over 80 percent. The company's executives were delighted with the results. They were so pleased that they promoted Susan, expanding her management role and giving her a substantial pay raise. Customer Service was now seemingly being managed by a person called to the management profession.

Given Susan's progress, it came as a great surprise when she abruptly resigned. During her exit interview, she expressed her disdain at being thrust into having to manage her department. Susan commented, "The people I was expected to manage were my friends. These were people I had worked with as a fellow customer service representative for years. After my promotion to manager, nothing much really changed. We still continued as friends and everyone seemed to be doing a good job. But that all changed when I was given a system for managing my department. Now I was asked to measure and manage my employees' performance. I enjoyed my job when there were no performance expectations and I could simply be friends with everyone. But I now see that was not managing. And frankly, being a manager is not a job I am interested in doing. I've taken an hourly job with another company where I don't have to manage anyone."

Despite Susan's management success, she did not have the aptitude to thrive as a manager. It was more important to Susan to be liked than to manage her employees. In the short term, Susan proved a good student in successfully practicing the management disciplines. However, over time, it turned out managing was not Susan's calling, as her heart was never in it. Sadly, it is not the case for many in management today.

A manager's ability to obtain successful results only clouds the reality that the manager's heart is not in his or her work— that the manager does not in fact have a management calling. In the same way, a manager's inability to obtain success clouds whether he or she also possess management aptitude.

An example of this was a manger named Tony, who was employed as a production supervisor at a southeastern manufacturing plant that made automobile starters and generators. Tony's plant had been losing $100,000 a month for the past eighteen months (on annual sales of $6 million).

The company's owner had heard of my turnaround work and asked to meet me. During the meeting, the owner acknowledged that I was not the first consultant he had called. In fact, he already had several expert opinions as to what to do about his company. The other experts had all arrived at the same conclusion: close the company. This was based on concluding the company's business model was flawed beyond repair, its operations "systemically unprofitable," and its management team (including Tony) "incompetent—incapable of effectively managing the company's resources."

However, the owner had misgivings about abruptly closing the plant. He had owned the business for many years and came to admire the hardworking men and women who he knew depended on the company for their livelihoods. He wanted to be sure closing the plant was the right decision. He wanted one more opinion. That is why he asked to meet me, to have me confirm whether he should close the company. If not, going forward he wanted a realistic alternative to make the company profitable. He gave me a week to give him an answer.

My consulting team and I spent that week delving into how the company was operated and managed. Two facts quickly became obvious. One fact was the company had too many employees who produced too few starters and alternators to make a profit. It took 275 employees to produce 5,000 units per week. To make a profit, the company would need to get down to 125 employees who could produce the same 5,000 units. Producing 5,000 units with 125 employees instead of the current 275 employees was a daunting prospect. It was one that no doubt influenced the experts in making the recommendation they did.

The second fact was that management was not practicing the learned disciplines of management. Whether the experts saw this as a factor I cannot say, but they had obviously seen the results of this neglect, as Tony and his fellow managers struggled to produce 5,000 units a week with the employees they had. The experts questioned how this beleaguered and inept management team could manage to produce the same number of units with significantly less employees. They concluded that they couldn't do it.

But were these experts correct? Was the business "systemically unprofitable," and were Tony and his management colleagues inept? Appearances suggested so.

However, as the week wound down, we obtained answers to these questions that belied appearances. Our analysis highlighted a positive possibility. If the plant employees' productivity could be increased to 70 percent, the company could make a profit. Of course, this meant that the management team had to maximize resources and results through effective problem solving. We knew from past experience that practicing the learned disciplines of management made this entirely possible (in fact, obtaining an 80 percent productivity level was likely). Based on this analysis, we concluded the business was viable and certainly not systemically unprofitable.

But were the experts correct about the company's management team being incapable of managing effectively? Presently this was all too true. Without exception, the plant's management team was particularly inept. We estimated that the productivity of the plant's various departments was currently around 30 percent.

But was Tony and his management colleagues' failure to make the right things happen a true reflection on their ability to manage effectively? We had no way to answer this question except through a grand experiment. The test would be simple: give the plant's management the tools they needed to manage effectively, and then stand back and see if they could. I wasn't too sure this was an experiment the owner would be anxious to adopt, but it was the only one we had.

Over the course of the week, we developed a turnaround plan. When the week concluded, the plan's central tenet was to make management more effective through a system for management employing the seven learned disciplines of management. If the company's management could skillfully use these tools, the company was theoretically fixable.

However, making management more effective was not a given, but a theory. Management's failure could indeed be because of their not having the aptitude to manage. If the experts were right on this point, the company would continue to lose money regardless of its theoretical potential.

Although we did not have answers to all our questions, we did have enough information to offer an alternative to closing the company.

The following week, we met with the owner. I began, "Theoretically, the plant can be operated profitably. To accomplish this, we would have to produce the same number of units per week with 125 employees instead of the current 275 employees. This would mean that management would have to manage the remaining employees' productivity to a 70 percent performance level."

I continued, "One reason the plant's employees' productivity is so low is that your management team is not practicing fundamental management disciplines. The first step in addressing this problem is to develop, design, and deploy a system for managing. Once the system is deployed, your management team would have the necessary tools to manage effectively. This first step would take our consulting team four weeks to complete.

"Not having the tools to effectively manage is one reason for the poor results, but it may not be the only one. It may be, as the experts concluded, that your management team is incapable of managing. If this is the case, giving them the tools won't help. It is one thing to say the company can be managed more effectively and profitably and another thing to actually do it.

"The critical question is, can the plant's management team effectively manage once they are given the tools to do so?

Unfortunately, we don't know the answer to this question and we won't know the answer unless we try.

"An attempt to turn around the company would take approximately ninety days—if all goes according to plan. The plan hinges on deploying and management capably using the learned disciplines of management. If your management team has this capability, a successful turnaround is at hand. If not, more of your money will be lost."

"I don't want to close the plant," the owner said. "Let's give it a try. But at the first indication that our management team does not have what it takes, I want you to let me know so I can cut my losses."

"Sure," I replied. "We will give you weekly progress reports so you will know where things stand."

With that, the meeting ended and we drove to the plant to carry out the turnaround plan. After four weeks, we deployed the learned disciplines of management throughout the company's various departments. Now management had the tools to make the right things happen.

A major layoff ensued as we got down to 125 employees. We told the remaining employees, "We believe we have all the people we need to produce 5,000 units per week. If we are right, the company can make a profit. We'll give it a try next week. We will need your help so that we can work smarter, faster, cheaper, and better. Please let us know how we can help you, especially in solving the problems that hinder your performance. See you Monday morning."

The following Monday, we began practicing the learned disciplines of management. I'll never forget Tony's actions. In an effort to prod his assemblers into attempting to hit their seemingly impossible production schedules (which was over double the amount they had ever done), Tony was passing out $20 bills. This was money out of his own pocket, as incentive, to get his assemblers to attempt the impossible. Try it they did, as 125 assemblers produced 5,200 units that first week.

Over the following weeks, we continued to solve problems while maintaining comparable production levels, and by month's end, the plant had made a profit—its first profitable month in a year and a half. In the coming months, Tony and his management team not only broke every production record in the firm's twenty-year history but also continued to build on that record, establishing a new industry-wide manufacturing productivity record. This was hardly the result of an inept management team. Despite appearances, the experts had been wrong about Tony and his fellow managers.

The failures of Tony and the plant's other managers had hidden their management aptitude. Once they had the tools to manage effectively, they were able to make the right things happen, effectively turning around their troubled company.

As these examples illustrate, a manager's seeming success or failure does not always provide an accurate arbiter of management aptitude. Nevertheless, for those men and women who aspire to manage, it is essential that their management aptitude be confirmed so that they can rightly assume their true vocational calling. It is a vital calling that plays a central role in an organization's success.

Peter Drucker emphasized management's contribution to an organization's success when he stated, "Management is the organ of institutions, the organ that converts a mob into an organization, and human efforts into performance."[2] Indeed, when management is effectively practiced, managers can make the right things happen, thus sustaining organizational success. This success can mean the difference between a profit and a loss, prosperity and decline, having a job and having to look for one.

So let's ask the question that we began this chapter with: Are you called—uniquely gifted and irresistibly drawn—to the management profession?

To help you answer this question, we'll conclude with seven specific management attributes that I believe validate one's management aptitude:

1. Desire. Managers have an inexplicable urge or desire to lead, to take charge, to control the outcome and be responsible for making the right things happen. This desire is not contrived but is innate, a natural outpouring of one's calling.

2. Fulfillment. Managing is fulfilling to those called to the profession. Managers find more satisfaction in managing activities than in doing the activities themselves. Therefore, delegating is second nature to them, so the work gets done and done more effectively and efficiently. Managers find satisfaction in producing excellent results while working with and through others.

3. Mind-set. A manager's mind is always actively managing, constantly looking for ways to manage more effectively. Managers are constantly thinking, analyzing, critiquing, evaluating, and observing how to better use resources and how to obtain greater results.

4. Intellect. Managers are able to envision an activity's processes, methods, and procedures. As a result, they are able to assess if resources and results are being maximized and when they are not to optimally organize them.

5. Caring. Managers care for people. This engenders respect and trust. People thrive when they feel cared for—knowing they will be treated fairly. Caring managers motivate and empower employees to join them in making the right things happen.

6. Focus. Managers have the ability to focus on the most important operational aspects. They possess the judgment and discipline to concentrate on the part or parts most critical to success while avoiding secondary distractions. Focus enables a manager to maximize

resources and results.

7. Action-oriented. Management is an action-oriented profession, and managers are predisposed to act. When the wrong things happen, a manager instinctively takes action to obtain the desired outcome. Managers are motivated, driven with a sense of urgency to take action to make the right things happen.

# Appendix B
# Typical Departmental Performance Ratios

Here are some typical departmental ratios often added to the Daily Performance Summary.

**Sales**

- The requested number of sales quotes stated as a percentage of the total number of sales calls made (with sales calls not leading to a quote treated as a problem on the Daily Performance Report)

- The number of sales orders generated stated as a percentage of the total number of sales quotes requested (with sales quotes not converted to a sales order treated as a problem on the Daily Performance Report)

- Individual salesperson's sales closing percentage

- Average number of sales calls required to make a sale

**Manufacturing**

- Documented problems frequency ranking

- The average actual time it takes to produce one unit

- Defect percentage by individual or manufacturing process

**Maintenance and Technical Service**

- Maintenance hours performed as a ratio to downtime

- The number of repeat service requests stated as a percentage of total service calls by individual technician

- Average actual time required to complete a service call

**Procurement**

- Individual buyer's compliance ratio to vendor quotes objectives
- Individual buyers cost reductions ratio to total purchases
- Ratio of items substituted due to stock-outs (documented as a problem on the Daily Performance Report)

**Distribution**

- Percent of on-time deliveries
- Percent adherence to stock being strategically located
- The average actual time required to process one order

**Engineering**

- Percent reduction in processing time
- The number of repeated change orders requests stated as a percentage of the total number of change orders by responsible engineer
- Average actual engineering hours per process

**Accounting**

- Percent of invoices disputed (documented as problems on the Daily Performance Report)
- Ratio of successful past-due account follow-ups compared to total follow-ups
- Cost ratio of accounting policy noncompliance

**Customer Service**

- Customer survey satisfaction ratio

- Customer complaints as a percentage of total customer orders

- Percentage of customer orders that could not be fulfilled (also recorded as a problem on the Daily Performance Report)

# Notes

## Introduction

1. Peter F. Drucker, Management Tasks, Responsibilities, Practices (New York, NY: Butterworth-Heineman, 1974), 11.
2. Merriam-Webster Online, s.v. "management," accessed April, 2012, http://www.merriam-webster.com/dictionary/management.
3. Carl von Clausewitz, On War (London, 1873), 40.
4. David Maraniss, When Pride Still Mattered (New York, NY: Simon & Schuster, 1999), 274.
5. Ibid., 58.
6. Thucydides, The History of the Peloponnesian War, Benjamin Jowett, translator (Oxford, England, 1900), Vol. 1, 58.

## Chapter 1

1. Twelve O'Clock High, directed by Henry King (Twentieth Century Fox Film, 1949).
2. Yogi Berra, Dave Kaplan, When You Come To a Fork in the Road, Take It! (New York, NY: Hyperion, 2001), 53.
3. David Stout, "Back on Capitol Hill, U.S. auto executives still find skeptics", New York Times, December 4, 2008.

## Chapter 2

1. Plutarch, Plutarch's Lives of Illustrious Men, Vol. II (Rockville, MD: Wildside Press, 2007), 290.
2. Taiichi Ohno, "Ask 'why' five times about every matter.", released on March, 2006, http://www.toyota-global.com/company/toyota_traditions/quality/mar_apr_2006.html.

## Chapter 3

1. Cristina M. Giannantonio, Ph.D., Amy E. Hurley-Hanson, Ph.D., "Frederick Winslow Taylor: Reflections on the Relevance of The Principles of Scientific Management100 Years Later", Journal of Business and Management 17, no. 1 (2011), 8.
2. Frederick Taylor, The Principles of Scientific Management (New York, NY: W. W. Norton & Company, Inc.), 1967.
3. "What gets measured gets done.", Tom Peters, released on April 1986, http://www.tompeters.com/column/1986/005143.php.
4. Susan Herrington, Survey Work Satisfaction (Clarksville, TN: North Tennessee Private Industry Council, 2010).

## Chapter 4

1. Phillip S. Meilinger, "When the Fortress Went Down," Air Force Magazine, October 2004.
2. As quoted in John Drescher, Triumph of Good Will: How Terry Sanford Beat a Champion of Segregation and Reshaped the South (Jackson, MS, University Press of Mississippi, 2000), 272.

## Chapter 5

1. Wikipedia Online, s.v. "W. Edwards Deming ," accessed April, 2012, http://www. http://www.wikipedia.org/.
2. Dan Close, Early Airmail Pilots Risked Life and Limb, November 1984, http://www.wingsoverkansas.com/history/article.asp?id=106.

## Chapter 6

1.   Carlo D'Este, Patton: A Genius for War,(New York, NY: Harper Perennial, 1996), 665.
2.   Niccolò Machiavelli, The Prince (New York, NY: Bantam, 1984).

## Chapter 7

1.   Administrative Office of the United States Courts, Statistical Tables 2006-2010 (five year average), November 2010, http://www.uscourts.gov/.
2.   Plato, Meno, Edited by Reginald Allen, Greek Philosophy (New York, NY: Free Press, 1966), 128.
3.   Ron Chernow, Washington: A Life (New York, NY: Penguin, 2010), 49
4.   "Ask 'why' five times about every matter.", Taiichi Ohno, released on March, 2006, http://www.toyotaglobal.com/company/toyota_traditions /quality/ mar_apr_2006.html.

## Appendix A

1.   William Tecumseh Sherman, Memoirs of Gen. William T. Sherman (New York, NY: D. Appleton & Company, 1891), 2:407.
2.   Peter Drucker, Managing In Turbulent Times (New York: HarperCollins 1980), 226.

# INDEX

Administration, 22
Accounting, 22, 79, 161-162, 211
Actionable Feedback, 135
Airmail Service, 115-116
AT&T, 198
Aviation Industry, 98, 115
Audit, 90-91
Auto Parts Manufacturer, 124

Bankrupt, 154
Baseball, 67-68
Berra, Yogi, 25
Best Practices, 83
Bethlehem Steel, 65
Beverage Operations, 21
Boeing, 99-102
  model B-17, 102
  model 299, 99-102
  flying fortress, 99, 102
Building Components Manufacturing, 21

Call Center, 36-39
Canada, 21
Cell Subassembly Department, 7-15, 56-58, 83-86
Checklist, 98, 103-103, 127
Chemical Refinishing, 22
Chrysler, 124-125
Clausewitz, Carl von, 4
Commercial Furniture, 95-97
Commercial Products Company, 161
Computer Manufacturing, 22
Construction, 22
Construction Blueprint, 26
Consumer Products, 45
Corporate Turnaround Consulting, Inc., 18
Cost Benefit Analysis, 160, 163, 167
Courier Delivery Services, 22
Customer service, 22, 48, 77, 86, 116, 200-202, 211

Daily Performance Report, 104, 139
Daily Performance Summary, 140-144, 150, 210
Deming, W. Edwards, 114
Design, 22
Distribution (consumer and industrial), 22, 90, 211
Douglas, 99-100
Drucker, Peter, 2, 207

Electrical Equipment Manufacturing, 22
Electronic Equipment Manufacturing, 22
Engineering, 22, 150-151, 211
English Proverb, 42
Equal Employment Opportunity Commission, 78
Equation for Management effectiveness, 40
Europe, 17, 21
Executing, 92, 93-113, 150, 173, 191
  assigning activities, 97
  checklist, 97-105
  empowering employees, 98
  engaging employees, 97
  four aspects of, 97
  practice of, 108-113
  ineffectively practiced, 94-97
Exercise Equipment Manufacturing, 22, 50

Final Assembly, 14, 96, 163
Following Up, 93, 96, 113, 114-133, 139, 147, 150-151, 155, 173, 192
  actionable feedback, 114-121, 127
  align activities, 122-123
  flying by the seat of pants, 115-121
  instill cooperation and foster accountability, 123-124
  practicalities of, 127-130
  typical scenarios, 130
  reinforce making the right things happen, 124-126
Forklift, 58-61
Fortune 500 Company, 7, 15, 18, 21
Fulfillment, 22
Furniture Manufacturing, 22

General Motors, 27-28
Gergen, David, 93, 105
Gourmet Food Purveying, 22
Green Bay Packers, 5

Heart Pacemaker Manufacturer, 163
Higher Education, 22
Hill, Ployer P., 100-101

218    Index

Industrial Packaging, 116
Industrial Sales Company, 58
Industrial X-ray, 163-166
Inventory Bin Location, 59-60

Lombardi, Vince, 5, 6

Machiavelli, 134, 136
Maintenance, 22, 46, 210
Management (definition), 2
Management Consulting, 7, 15, 16
Manufacturing, 22, 210
Marketing, 22
Martin, 99
Measuring Performance, 63, 64-92, 93-94, 96, 150, 155, 173
  administrator, 90-91
  correcting wrong measures, 89-90
  facilitates management practice, 70-71
  how to, 82-89
  ideal performance measure, 82, 85
  negative perceptions, 72-82
  outcome based measures, 69, 87-89
  relational based measures, 69-70
  three ways to measure, 69
  time based measures, 69, 83-87

  what is, 68
  why it is not practiced, 71-72
Medical Device Manufacturing, 22
Medical Pathologist, 21
Metal Cutting, 50-53
Metal Fastener Manufacturing, 28
Metal Stamping, 22
Murphy's Law, 4

Ohno, Taiichi, 54, 159
Oil and Gas Refining, 22
Organizational Change, 146
Organizing, 41, 42-63, 93-94, 96, 150, 188
  evaluating organization, 54-57
  optimally organizing activities, 57-61
  organize around most valuable resources, 62
  recognize the activities, 43-49
  understand the activity, 49-53

Pareto Principle, 60
Patton, George, 134-135
Peters, Tom, 64, 66
Performance Reports (see Reports)
Piston Ring Manufacturing, 22
Planning, 23-41, 93-95, 150, 181
  essential elements, 26

## Index

right aims, 28
right means, 38
specific and measurable aims, 30
specific and measurable means, 39
wrong aims, 26
wrong means, 36
Plutarch, 42-43
Primordial Swamp, 154
Private Company, 21
Problem Solving, 93, 97, 153, 154-169, 173, 192
  is problem worth solving, 160-162
  monitor problem, 167-168
  recognize, identify and under stand problem, 156-160
  taking action on problem, 166-167
  which problem solution to implement, 163-166
Procurement, 22, 211
Public Company, 21
Public Utilities, 22, 47
Publishing, 22, 76
Purchasing, 47, 49, 126
Puritans, 196

Quality assurance, 22

Railroad Tank Car Refurbishing, 22

Reagan, Ronald, 76
Real-time Reporting, 93, 96, 133, 134-153, 155, 157, 161-162, 167-168, 173
  distributes performance information, 138-143
  essentials, 136
  facilitates problem solving, 153
  identifies best practices, 152-153
  links management practice, 149-152
  not accounting information, 137-138
  perpetuates ideal performance, 145-149
  structures follow-up meetings, 143-145
Rebuild It (fictional company), 171-194
Reformation, 196
Reports, 104, 141-142
  daily performance report, 104
  daily performance summary, 141
  weekly performance summary, 142
Restaurant Operations, 22
Retail Operations, 22

Sales, 22, 161-162, 210
Sherman, William T., 196, 199-200

# Index

Socrates, 154, 156
Software Developers, 87
Steel Processing, 22
Stock-outs, 48-49

Taylor, Frederick, 64-66
Technical Service Department, 80, 91, 210
Testing Equipment, 45
The Principles of Scientific Management, 64-66
Third Army, 134
Thucydides, 1, 19
Toyota, 54, 107, 159
Toyota Production System, 54
Transportation, 22

Trench Foot, 134-135
Turbine Fin Manufacturer, 44
Twelve O'clock High, 23

United States, 17, 21
United States Postal Service, 115
U.S. Army Air Corps, 98-102
U.S. Army Eighth Air Force, 23
U.S. Third Army, 134-135

Wagner, Rich, 27-28
Warehouse, 58, 60
Washington, George, 156